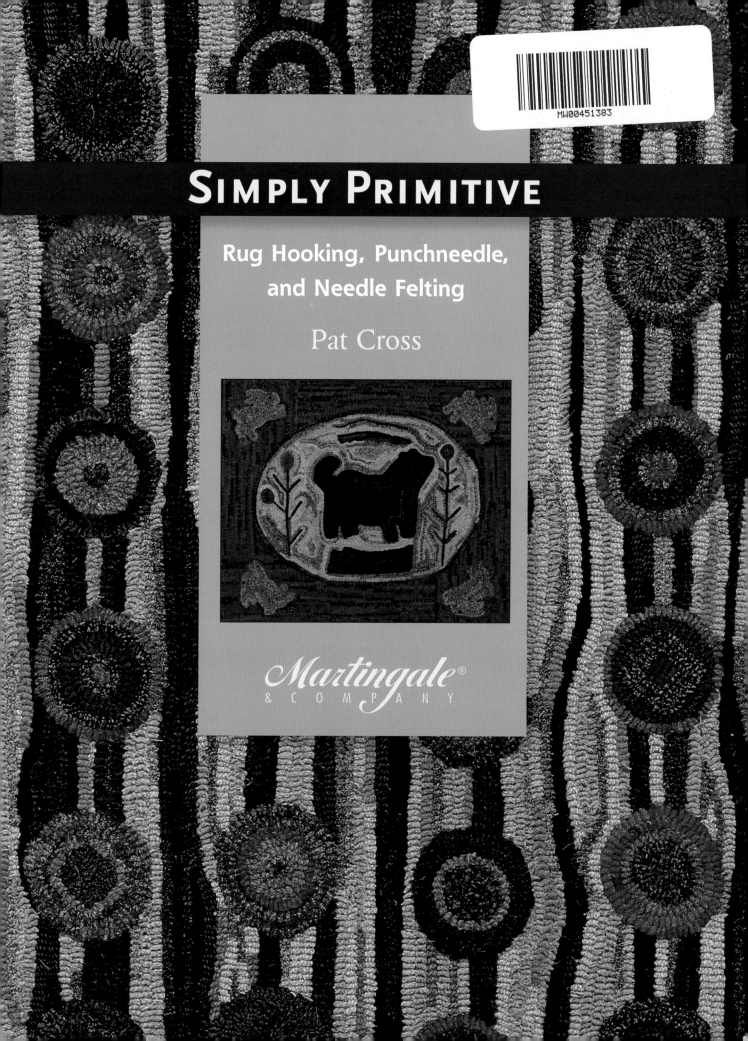

SIMPLY PRIMITIVE

Rug Hooking, Punchneedle, and Needle Felting

Pat Cross

Martingale®
& COMPANY

Simply Primitive:
Rug Hooking, Punchneedle, and Needle Felting
© 2006 by Pat Cross

That Patchwork Place® is an imprint of
Martingale & Company®.

Martingale & Company
20205 144th Avenue NE
Woodinville, WA 98072-8478 USA
www.martingale-pub.com

Credits

President .... Nancy J. Martin
CEO.. Daniel J. Martin
COO... Tom Wierzbicki
Publisher.. Jane Hamada
Editorial Director........................... Mary V. Green
Managing Editor............................ Tina Cook
Technical Editor............................. Karen Costello Soltys
Copy Editor .... Durby Peterson
Design Director .... Stan Green
Illustrator .... Laurel Strand
Cover and Text Designer.............. Stan Green
Photographer................................. Brent Kane

Mission Statement

Dedicated to providing quality products and service
to inspire creativity.

Dedication

This one is for Scout. Some will think I'm nuts and probably should dedicate this to my husband, Tom. He, more than anyone, understands how much we loved and miss that cat.

Printed in China
11 10 09 08 07 06   8 7 6 5 4 3 2 1

Library of Congress Cataloging-in-Publication Data

Library of Congress Control Number: 2006010773

ISBN-13 : 978-1-56477-657-0
ISBN-10 : 1-56477-657-3

CONTENTS

Hooked rug, framed punchneedle, and needle-felted pumpkins

What's in This Book?

Since writing *Purely Primitive: Hooked Rugs from Wool, Yarn, and Homespun Scraps* (Martingale & Company, 2003), I have had many new and experienced rug hookers encourage me to write another book. Yes, that's flattering, but my immediate thoughts were "Yeah, sure!" If only they knew the amount of work that goes into writing a book.

When I wrote *Purely Primitive*, I had no idea how it would affect my life. My goal in writing the book was to impart everything I had learned along the way. I have been very fortunate to attend many camps, workshops, and classes with top-notch teachers. Through writing and teaching, I can share those experiences with you. Since my first book, I've known that there is more I want to share with you, but fear can be crippling. Fear? Yes, fear. *Purely Primitive* is a good book. At least that is what so many have told me. How would I follow that? I knew that if I did another book, I didn't want it to be just a pattern book. I wanted it to be a continuing education in rug hooking. So let me tell you what I'd like to share with you this time.

People have asked me how I go about designing rugs. Where do I get my ideas, and what inspires me? I won't give away all my secrets, but I'll tell you enough to get your creative juices flowing. I'm also often asked about my color palette and how I mix so much similar-colored wool and make it work. I'll explain this with a rug that is hooked in only two colors but uses more than a dozen values of as-is wool, wool that is used as is without being overdyed by the rug hooker. There is also a chapter dedicated to the questions I am asked most often when I teach. Some questions address general things that I cover in the principles of rug hooking, and others are curiosities about my particular way of doing things.

This book also shows you how I go about entertaining myself when I'm not working on a rug. My hands are almost never idle. I love to quilt and do counted cross-stitch, especially antique-looking samplers. Two of my more recent ventures have taken me into punchneedle embroidery and needle felting. I find both are great stress relievers! Once I explain the process, you'll see how all that punching and poking are good for releasing all those pent-up anxieties.

Needle felting and punchneedle are also very complementary to rug hooking. Needle felting gives me another excuse to buy wool. This time it's wool roving. Wool roving can be dyed and used in a couple of different ways. My favorite is making three-dimensional items. Punchneedle lets me make miniature hooked rugs. I like to frame my punchneedle pieces and hang them on walls. Rug hooking, needle felting, and punchneedle can all be done using warm, muted colors and very similar designs and patterns to achieve that antique, primitive look I love. So if hooking a rug, needle punching a miniature rug, or sculpting a three-dimensional felted item appeals to you, you're likely to find some exciting projects here.

THE EQUIPMENT AND MATERIALS needed to hook a rug can be simple and inexpensive or elaborate and more costly. It's like buying a car. You can purchase a VW Beetle or a Rolls-Royce. They will both get you there, but they offer very different experiences for your journey.

If you are a first-time rug hooker, I'd suggest starting with the least expensive equipment. Find out if you like this fiber art before you invest a lot of money. If you get truly hooked, I'd suggest trying other people's equipment before you purchase your own. Be sure to investigate all your options before you buy something that someone tells you is the only way to go. Rug-hooking equipment is personal. What works for someone else may not be what's comfortable for you.

In the discussion that follows, I list the equipment needed from simple and least expensive to the more elaborate and costly.

Hoops and Frames

For a beginner, I'd suggest a 14" wooden quilting hoop. You want a quilting hoop, not an embroidery hoop. Quilting hoops are deep enough to hold your backing taut, and they allow you to turn the hoop as you work, which may be a plus if you're comfortable hooking in one direction only.

Hoops also fit on various stands; some are propped in your lap, others stand on the floor. Hoops have two advantages—low price and

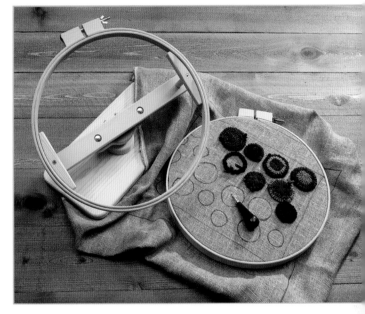

Quilting hoops

portability. If you prefer using a hoop, you may want to purchase a longer bolt to accommodate the bulk of your rug. This is especially helpful if you're working with ¼"-wide or wider strips.

Purchasing a rug-hooking frame is like buying a piece of furniture. Frames come in all sizes, colors, and shapes. They can be propped in your lap, fitted to a simple floor frame, or attached to an elaborate floor frame that can accommodate your cutter, scissors, a lamp, and any other accessory you can think of. They are made out of pine, oak, maple, or aluminum. Yes, the latest to hit the market, the Townsend Orbiter, is made from lightweight, aircraft-grade aluminum!

You can also make a very simple frame by nailing four wood slats together to form a square or rectangle. You can then use thumbtacks or push pins to hold the backing in place.

Frames with little metal teeth or prongs, known as gripper strips, are the ones most widely used. Very simple lap frames; collapsible, heavy-duty plastic frames; and more elaborate frames usually have gripper strips.

Frames with gripper strips

To explore the options, I'd suggest purchasing a copy of *Rug Hooking* magazine to check out the advertisements showing rug-hooking frames. The Internet, shops, rug-hooking guilds, and camps are other places where you can look at the various frames available.

Cutters

Cutting wool into strips requires a cutter. If you're a beginner who has been a quilter, try the rotary cutter you already have. However, I wouldn't cut strips narrower than ¼" wide with a rotary cutter; it's too hard to maintain accuracy. Another option for beginners is to purchase a kit with precut strips.

Cutters all cut wool in a variety of strip widths—$^2/_{32}$" to ½"—but they vary from a simple tabletop model to a sophisticated piece of machinery like the Townsend Fabric Cutter, and prices vary accordingly from about $150 to over $400.

Strip Size	Strip Width
2	$^2/_{32}$" ($^1/_{16}$")
3	$^3/_{32}$"
4	$^4/_{32}$" (⅛")
5	$^5/_{32}$"
6	$^6/_{32}$" ($^3/_{16}$")
7	$^7/_{32}$"
8	$^8/_{32}$" (¼")
8.5	$^{10}/_{32}$" ($^5/_{16}$")
9	$^{12}/_{32}$" (⅜")
10	$^{16}/_{32}$" (½")

Cutters come in two styles—tabletop and clamp-on. There are several manufacturers of the clamp-on models. Fraser, maker of the Bliss tabletop cutter, also makes the 500-1 clamp-on model. Rigby offers clamp-on cutters, and one of their models can accommodate two cutter blades. Bolivar, a Canadian manufacturer, offers a clamp-on model that has three pre-installed cutter heads. The Townsend, a clamp-on cutter, comes with one cutter head (known as a cartridge), and additional cutter heads can be purchased.

Townsend clamp-on cutter

My personal experience with these cutters includes all but the Rigby. I started with a Bliss tabletop cutter. It's the most economical. You never have to find a table edge to clamp it onto, and changing the cutter blades is easy. When I started making kits, I purchased a Fraser 500-1, clamp-on model. The handles on clamp-on cutters are much larger. With each handle rotation, you cut a longer strip, which definitely increases your production.

I've never owned a Rigby cutter, but I know many people who do, and they swear by them. They're priced similarly to the Fraser 500-1.

My next purchase was a Bolivar clamp-on cutter. It costs more than the Fraser or Rigby, but it comes with three pre-installed blades.

After the Bolivar, I bought the Townsend. It's an unbelievably great cutter, but pricey. It's made in the USA, service is top notch, and changing the cartridges (blades) is simple and fast! Of all the cutters I have owned, the Townsend is the easiest to operate. Changing the cartridge takes only a few seconds and requires no tension adjustments.

Other cutter models are available. One is even electrically operated. But I can only vouch for the ones that I've owned and used (Bliss, Fraser 500-1, Bolivar, and Townsend).

Hooks

In the early days of rug hooking, a hook was often a bent nail imbedded in a piece of wood. Hooks have come a long way since then. You can now find any size, style, color, or exotic wooden handle you can imagine. The one thing I can't stress enough is this: find a hook that fits your hand and is comfortable to use.

For a beginner, I suggest a simple Moshimer hook. They are inexpensive, come in fine, medium, coarse, and primitive hook sizes, and fit most hands comfortably. After you have hooked a while, I suggest you try other hooks. Many primitive rug hookers prefer the Hartman hook. It's a high-quality hook made in Ireland. The shaft of the hook is chunky, thus making a nice, wide opening in your rug backing to pull your wool strip through.

Hooks come in different sizes. You need a fine hook when you hook with narrow strips (#3 or #4). A medium hook is suitable for slightly wider strips (#5 or #6), and a coarse or primitive hook is best for hooking with wider strips (#7 and up).

Hooks come in various handle styles, too, such as ergonomic, ball, or pencil. You need to

Variety of hooks

Backings or Foundations

To hook your rug, you'll need a foundation or backing to pull your wool strips through. There are four different backings—burlap, monk's cloth, rug warp, and linen. Scottish burlap, monk's cloth, and primitive linen are the most common backings used for hooking primitive rugs. Rug warp is a cotton backing that is similar to monk's cloth but is heavier and more tightly woven. Therefore, rug warp is best used in conjunction with a smaller cut (narrower strips) because the tight weave makes it more difficult to pull wide strips of wool through.

The burlap sold today is nothing like the burlap you'll see on the backs of old rugs. It's far more durable. Monk's cloth is an even weave of 100% cotton. Linen is the most expensive backing, but many say it's the most durable. At one time there was only primitive linen available, but now there are several different primitive linens to choose from. My linen of choice is what some people refer to as "hairy" linen. It's off-white to ecru in color, and it does not have an even weave like monk's cloth. When I order linen I request Scottish primitive linen.

find a hook that fits your hand. Each person's hands are unique in size and strength. So that you don't develop any physical problems with your hooking hand, try several different models and use the one that works best for you.

The best thing you can do for your hooking career is to find a hook that fits your hand, and then match the hook size with the strip size and backing fabric. Using a fine hook to pull ¼" strips through a primitive linen backing is just as difficult as using a primitive Hartman hook to pull a #3 cut strip through rug warp. Be kind to your hands.

From left to right: monk's cloth, burlap, and primitive linen are examples of backings used in primitive rug hooking.

Backings are another one of those things that are personal. Some prefer monk's cloth because it's soft and clings to a frame easily. Others choose burlap because of its low price, and there are those who love hairy linen because it's easy to pull wide strips through, and it's durable. Try them all and decide which you like best.

Wool

In my world, *Wool* is a capital-letter word. Wool is one of nature's best products. It's soft, strong, supple, and very resilient. Ideally, you want to use 100%-wool fabric for rug hooking. New wool is better than old, recycled wool because it doesn't show signs of wear and has never been cleaned with chemicals.

Look for flannel-weight wool when you are shopping for quality wool for your rugs. Think of the old, pleated wool skirts many of us used to wear, and aim for that weight. A yard of flannel-weight wool weighs about 12 ounces. A slightly heavier weight is okay, but you don't want coat-weight wool or heavy wool blankets that are better used for rug braiding. You also don't want gabardine or worsted wool, which not only are the wrong weight but also tend to be stiff and shred easily.

Many people love to hunt for recycled wool in thrift stores. A great find is a large pleated skirt. Recycled wool must be washed and disassembled, and you need to discard all worn areas.

There are a couple of tests you can use to determine if the fabric is 100% wool. The burn test requires that you take a couple of threads (one from each direction in the weave) and put a match to it. If it is wool, it will smell like burned hair. Another test is the bleach test. Place a small piece of wool into a glass dish and cover it with liquid bleach. If it's 100% wool, it will dissolve within 24 hours. If there are any fibers left, it's probably a blend. If the original piece is still there after 24 hours, it's not wool.

Wool blends are okay to use. Sometimes that perfect color just happens to be a blend. If you

Swatches of various wool textures and bundles of dyed wool

must use blends, try and shoot for no less than 80% wool. Blends aren't as resilient, don't repel dirt, and don't dye as well as 100% wool.

When shopping for wool for primitive rugs, look for wool with texture, such as plaids, herringbones, heathers, checks, and paisleys. Old paisley shawls are a wonderful find, but the wool tends to be thin and fragile, so use it sparingly. Textures add charm and character, which makes a new rug appear older than it really is. Textures can also add shading and movement.

Washing and Storing Wool

Wool is your creative palette, and you should care for it that way. All wool stops in my laundry room before it goes into my wool stash. It is washed and dried before I store it. I like knowing that when I pull wool off the shelf for a rug, it's been washed and is ready to be used.

Why wash it? Wool is like any other pro-cessed fiber—it has sizing in it. It's also flat and ugly looking. Compare a swatch of wool before and after it has been washed. The transformation is amazing. It boggles my mind that a box containing 20 yards of unwashed wool appears to double in size after it has been washed. During the washing process the fibers tighten and fluff, which is referred to as *fulling* or *felting.*

Washed and unwashed wool swatches

Over the years I have come to find that it's not the temperature of washing and drying the wool that fulls it, but the agitation. I wash and rinse all my wool in cold water. I dry it on a permanent-press cycle with a fabric-softener sheet.

Each washing machine is different, and I can't offer advice regarding those new washers that have no agitator in the center. What works for me is the following: If it's flannel-weight wool, I'll wash it on a regular 12-minute cycle. If it's a bit thinner, I'll wash it on a regular cycle for 15 minutes. If it's perfect the way it is, I'll wash it on a delicate 6-minute cycle. When in doubt, always start with a shorter agitation time. It's better to have to rewash the wool than to ruin it by overwashing it and shrinking it too much.

The best way to store wool is on open shelves and out of direct sunlight. Having this luxury is not always possible. What you don't want to do is store wool in plastic bags or containers that are directly exposed to sunlight or heat. Con-densation forms in this type of environment and can lead to mold and eventually rotting. If you store your wool in plastic tubs or boxes, keep them out of direct light and away from heat.

We must be careful to avoid moths as well. To steer clear of them, start with a clean storage area and only store clean, washed wool there.

Preparing the Backing

For a more pleasant hooking experience, prepare your backing or foundation and get your pattern drawn straight on the grain before you pull your first loop. Here is how to do that.

Cut a piece of backing fabric a minimum of 4" wider on each side than the pattern. If your project is 20" x 30", then you'll need a piece of backing fabric at least 28" x 38". You'll need this extra backing so that your pattern will fit easily onto your frame or into a hoop.

I used to serge all the outer edges of my patterns to prevent them from fraying and raveling. If you don't have a serger, a simple zig-zag stitch using a regular sewing machine works great. If you don't have either, or don't want to take the time to set up your machine, masking tape or duct tape works beautifully, and I often use this on my backing edges. Folding a piece of 2"-wide masking tape over the raw edges of your pattern may not look pretty, but it works great, and eventually the tape will be cut off.

Draw along the straight of grain with a carpenter's pencil.

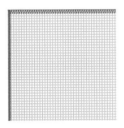

Serge or zigzag edges.

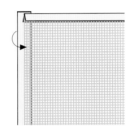

Tape edges.

Drawing the Pattern

Most of the patterns in this book require you to enlarge them before you can trace them onto the backing. You can take them to a facility (such as Kinko's) that will enlarge them the required percentage, or you can use large sheets of graph paper and draw them yourself following the enlarging ratio (such as 1 square = ½") printed on the pattern page.

Before you transfer the pattern, you need to make sure the outer edge of your pattern is aligned with the straight of the grain of the backing you're using. If you're using monk's cloth or rug warp, this is easy. These backings are woven evenly, so you just need to follow the straight-grain line. Primitive linen and burlap are more loosely woven, which makes it a little harder to follow a straight line. An easy way to get those lines straight is to use a wide-point pencil (a carpenter's pencil is great) and drag it in through the openings using firm pressure on the pencil.

For example, measure in 4" from the outer edge of your backing piece. Place the pencil in

one of the holes of the linen or burlap with your right hand (assuming you're right-handed) and pull the backing away from you with your left hand. The pencil should stay in the groove, and you should have an outside border line that is on the straight of the grain.

Continue this until all four outside border lines are drawn on the straight of the grain. Once the outside border lines are established, you need to sew a couple of stay-stitching rows approximately ¾" and 1" outside of the border line. You can do stay stitching with the zigzag stitch of a sewing machine or with a hand-sewn running stitch to prevent the backing from unraveling when you cut the excess backing away during the finishing process.

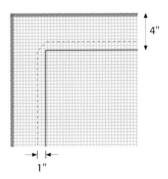

Stay-stitching

A simple way to transfer the pattern onto your squared-up backing is to use Red Dot Tracer, which can be found at most fabric stores. Red Dot is a lightweight, nonwoven fabric similar to interfacing, and it has red dots spaced 1" apart in a grid. These dots make it easy to align your pattern and keep it on the straight of grain.

Place a piece of Red Dot over the pattern you have enlarged. Make sure to line it up squarely on the pattern and trace the pattern onto the Red Dot. Now place the Red Dot on top of your backing piece, again making sure it's straight, and draw on your tracing lines with a heavy-duty, permanent black marker such as a Super Sharpie. This method will produce a light tracing of the pattern onto your backing. You may need to retrace the lines to make them bolder.

If you are using primitive linen, there is an easier way to transfer your pattern. Because of its light color and open weave, you can see through it pretty easily. Therefore, you can place your linen on top of the pattern and trace the pattern directly onto your linen.

How to Hook

These directions are for a right-handed person. If you're left-handed, simply reverse the directions.

1. Place the backing on your frame or in your hoop, making sure it is taut but not skin-tight. As a general rule, start hooking from the center of your rug and move toward the border. Hook just inside the black lines of the pattern.

2. Pick up the first strip with your left hand. Holding the strip between your thumb and forefinger, place your left hand underneath the backing.

3. With the hook in your right hand, push the end of the hook through an opening on the top of the backing. Place the wool strip in the curve of the hook and pull the end up through the hole so that about ½" shows on top of the backing. This is known as a *tail*.

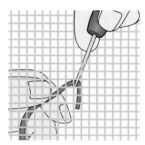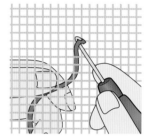

4. Place the hook into the very next hole and pull up the first loop. Use the hand underneath the backing to help guide the strip onto the hook so that it's not twisted, and pull the loop through the hole. Loops should be as high as the strip is wide. For instance, if you're using #8 strips, they're ¼" wide, so your loops should be ¼" high. When the loop is the right height, gently slide the hook out of the loop.

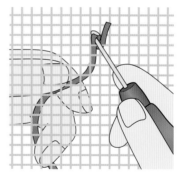

5. Continue pulling up loops in this same manner, inserting the hook into every second or third hole. This will vary depending on the thickness of your wool. You want the loops to touch each other but not be crammed together.

6. Continue pulling up loops until you are near the end of the wool strip. When you come to the end of the strip, just pull the end up through the hole. All strips begin and end on the topside. There should be no tails sticking out on the back.

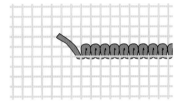

7. To start a new strip, insert the hook into the hole where the previous strip ended. Pull up the end of the next strip into that hole. There are now two tails in that hole. Pull up the next loop and continue. Stagger the starting and ending points from row to row. The tail ends will be less noticeable if they aren't all aligned.

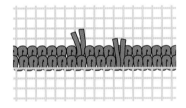

8. Occasionally, grasp the tails and clip them off to the height of the loops surrounding them.

Potential Challenges

Some shapes or portions of a rug can be trickier to hook than others. Here are some pointers to guide you.

Circles. Hooking circles is fun and easy, but sometimes they tend to form little mounds. To avoid this, start from the outside of the circle and work toward the center. It's particularly important that you do not cram your loops, and when you end in the center, a single tail will occupy a hole.

Corners. Try not to start or stop hooking in a corner; a full loop at a corner is stronger and looks

neater than two tails. To avoid tails at the corner, start and end a strip a few loops before the corner. Hook toward yourself along the edge. When you come to the corner, turn your frame so that you continue to hook toward yourself. Use your frame or hoop to make this task easy, and hooking corners shouldn't present problems.

Motifs. In most cases, hooking motifs is a two-step process: outline and fill. How you choose to hook a motif is entirely up to you. There are no rules, so make it the way you see it.

Backgrounds. Hooking backgrounds can be boring! The way to avoid this is to not leave it all until the end. After you hook each motif, surround it with at least one row of background wool. This will give you an idea of how the background will look and get you started on all that space that makes up a background.

My background hooking pattern of choice is what I call *meandering*. I do this because I think it adds interest and motion. To meander, take a permanent marker and draw a light wandering line through the background to divide the space. Hook on the line and use it as a guide for filling in the background.

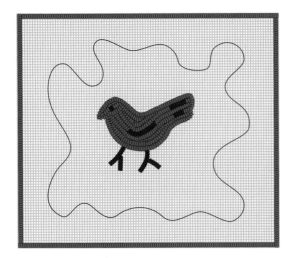

Directional hooking can be seen in many of the early primitive rugs, and I've always wondered why. Was it because the rug was on the frame in a stationary position and the maker was only comfortable hooking in one direction? Whatever the answer, it adds considerable charm to backgrounds of rugs. See the illustration below for some ideas.

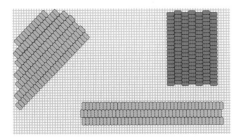

Finishing Your Rug

Once you've completed hooking your rug, you need to steam it and finish the edges. Two of the most popular ways of finishing the edges are with binding tape or by whipping the edges with wool yarn.

Steaming

For years I only steamed my rug after I had finished the edges. Now I steam it prior to finishing the edges and again after I have completed the entire rug. Steaming is an important step, and you'll be amazed at what good steaming can do for your rug's final appearance.

Steaming makes a rug lie flat and gives it a very finished look. Rugs hooked using monk's cloth tend to curl, and steaming will make the rug lie perfectly flat. Steaming can also help hide some imperfections in your hooking style.

The equipment needed for steaming a rug includes an ironing board, an iron, and a terry cloth towel. I usually use old dish towels. When I say steam, I'm not referring to ironing with a steam iron. I'm talking about using a dry iron, laying a damp terry cloth towel on top of the rug, and waiting until steam rises. The exact process is as follows.

Place the rug facedown on an ironing board. Place a towel that has been wet and wrung out on top of the rug. Place a dry iron on the damp towel and wait for steam to rise. This process usually takes 8 to 12 seconds. When you see steam rise, pick up the iron and move it to the next spot. Continue this process until the entire back is steamed. Then turn the rug over and repeat the process on the front. When you're completely done, lay the rug someplace where it can dry flat. This is a tedious process, especially if your rug is large, but it will give your rug that finished look.

As I mentioned before, I steam my rug before I do my edge-finishing work and then again after I've completed the work. Whether you're folding back the edge with binding tape or folding the edge for whipping, the steamed backing is softer and more pliable, which makes finishing the edges much easier.

Binding Tape

The easiest way to finish your rug is to use binding tape. Binding tape is available at rug-hooking specialty shops and through various mail-order sources. Binding tape is 1¼" wide, made of 100% cotton, and comes in many different colors. Try to match the color of the binding tape to the last row of hooking. If you can't match it perfectly, choose a color that is close in value.

To determine the amount of binding tape you'll need, measure the outside perimeter of your rug and add 12" for shrinkage allowance. Wash the binding tape before you apply it to your rug, because some colors bleed.

Binding tape can be sewn on before you start hooking or after you've made considerable progress. Just make sure you sew it on before you get close to the outside edge. If you wait to sew on binding tape until you're finished hooking the rug, it's much more difficult.

Place the tape on the top side of the backing so that the outer edge of the tape is aligned with the outer edge of the drawn pattern as shown. Sew by hand or machine, stitching as close to the edge as possible (no more than ⅛" seam). Ease the tape around the corner so that you'll be able to turn it to the back of the rug and miter the corner when the hooking is complete. If you don't want to miter the corners, you can sew a separate strip of binding tape to each side of the rug. If you do this, be sure to leave at least 1" extra at the ends of each strip for finishing.

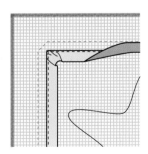

Hook the outside row as close as possible to the binding tape. When the hooking is complete, cut away the backing just beyond the stay stitching. Fold the binding back, miter the corners, and sew the binding tape to the back of the rug with heavy-duty thread.

Whipping

The term *whipping* means to wrap cording or the folded edge of the rug's backing with wool yarn using a whipstitch. A sturdy wool yarn will do, but I prefer Paternayan 3-ply wool needlepoint yarn. It is available in many colors and can usually be found at needlepoint shops. You'll need a tapestry needle with a large eye. If you choose to use cording, purchase ¼" to ⅜" cotton cording. This can usually be found in craft and fabric stores.

To estimate the yardage needed for whipping your rug, remember that a foot of yarn will cover about 1", and 1 yard covers 3". For example, a 24" x 36" rug has a perimeter of 120", so you'll need 120 feet or 40 yards of yarn to whip the edges.

Before you begin to whip, cut the excess backing just outside of the stay-stitching line. Place the cording on the top side of the rug next to the last row of hooking. Fold the backing over the cording to the back of the rug and pin it in place. Thread the tapestry needle with a piece of yarn about 36" long and whipstitch from top to bottom and right to left, working from the top side of the rug. Keep the whipping snug but not too tight. You don't need to knot the ends of the yarn. Bury the ends in the whipping yarn as you go.

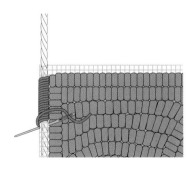

When whipping without cording, fold the backing over twice toward the top of the rug. Whip over this folded edge with the yarn. Again, keep the whipping snug but not too tight.

Final Steps

It's time to give your rug that final steaming. Don't stop now—do it one last time. It's also a good time to sew a label on your rug. A very simple way is to sew a light-colored piece of binding tape onto the back of your rug. Using a permanent-marking pen, write your name and the year you finished the rug on the binding tape.

If you have a fancy sewing machine, design a label especially for your rug. Some things you might consider adding to the label besides your name are the pattern name, the pattern designer, the year you finished the rug, and any other special details you want to remember.

Hooker's Hint: Rug Use

- Place a mesh, rubberized pad under rugs you have on the floor. This protects the rugs and prevents them from sliding, thus possibly preventing an accident.
- There are several ways to hang a rug on a wall. You can nail carpet-tack strips onto a wall and simply push the rug onto the prongs. You can sew a sleeve on the back of the rug and then hang it by using a dowel rod. Or you can mount a rug on a wooden frame and hang it. The size and weight of the rug will dictate the structure of the wooden frame. The larger and heavier the rug, the more support it will need. A simple wooden stretcher frame would be too flimsy for a rug of substantial size and weight. A frame is the best option when it comes to large, heavy rugs.
- When not in use, roll a rug so that the pretty, hooked side is facing out. This is just the opposite of how you might think it should be.

FREQUENTLY ASKED RUG-HOOKING QUESTIONS

WHEREVER I TEACH I always ask students to write down questions they may have about rug hooking. If I don't normally cover their topics in class, I make an effort to do so. These usually aren't how-to questions, but general curiosities about my way of doing things or my viewpoint on a topic. Below, I answer five of the questions that are asked most often.

1. What is "primitive"?

To me, primitive is a style. It's not based on the size strip you hook with or a specific pattern or design. There are six criteria that fit my interpretation of what primitive is:

1. Primitive designs are simple but heartwarming.

2. These designs have very little detail.

3. Muted, mellow, faded yet rich colors are used to hook these rugs.

4. The materials used most often are natural fibers: wool, cotton, silk, linen.

5. Primitive designs have no planned shading. If shading appears, it occurs merely because of the textured fibers used, such as plaids, tweeds, or herringbones.

6. Primitive designs often express something from within the designers or share a piece of their past.

Cat Birds hooked rug. This rug fits many of the criteria at left. It's simple and heartwarming, has no detail or shading, was hooked using as-is muted colors, and is whimsical without being too cute.

Primitives make me smile and wonder about the maker. Antique rugs from the period of 1860 to 1885 are the ones that appeal most to me. They show the work of untrained artists who expressed themselves by using whatever materials they had. That look is what I try to incorporate into my designs.

2. Where do I buy and how do I store wool?

I buy wool everywhere. I have an addiction. I can admit I have this addiction, but I'm not ready for a 12-step program. I don't buy wool with a certain rug in mind. Rather, when I see something I like, I buy it. I operate on the theory that I may never see it again, so buy it now.

Hooker's Hint: Buying Wool

- Buy what you like and buy it when you see it. There is no guarantee you'll be able to find it again.
- If you find wool you like, buy a yard. If you really like it, buy three yards. If it's a fabulous piece of wool that has many possibilities, buy five yards. Wool is the palette of your art.

Personally, I don't enjoy the hunt for recycled wool. I know lots of people who love that part of the game, but I'd rather be hooking than pawing through old clothes that still need to be taken apart before I can use them. I will not, however, pass up recycled wool that has already been taken apart, washed, and offered for sale.

So where do I find it all? In "Resources" on page 95, I have listed my favorite suppliers. There are others that I order from, and many of them advertise in *Rug Hooking* magazine. Other great sources are vendors at rug-hooking shows, hook-ins, or rug camps. Teachers are an excellent source; many sell wool during their classes.

Once you buy all the wool you like, storing it can present a challenge. Some people need to hide it from husbands. I've heard stories of hiding wool in the trunks of cars, under the bed, and any other place the spouse might not frequent. I'm fortunate that I don't have to hide it.

When I first got into rug hooking, my stash was limited and could fit nicely in a chimney cabinet that I had. Then I had a gorgeous workroom above a three-car garage, and I stored wool on open shelves that ran the length of one wall. Eventually I tried to get really organized, and I put the wool in purchased wire bins that slide out for easy access. I still use them, but they mostly hold dyed wool.

My favorite system is the one I'm using right now. I have what I call my wool room. It's a huge closet that measures 8 feet by 13 feet and has four 16"-deep shelves running along two walls. The wire bins with laminate tops mentioned above run along the other wall. Excellent lighting is essential for seeing the colors accurately, so I use full-spectrum or daylight bulbs in the overhead fluorescent light fixture.

In addition to the great lighting, I love that I can stand in the center of the room and look all around me to see what I have. Plus, there is floor space so that I can pull wool right there in the closet without having to take it to another room to really look at it. And finally, there's a door! It's my private space, and my wool is hidden from view.

Unfortunately, not everyone has a wool room. With whatever system you use, what you do need to remember is the following:

- Keep your wool out of bright sunlight.
- If you store your wool in plastic bins, don't store the bins near a heat source that can possibly cause condensation to form.
- Wash all your wool before you store it.

3. How do you know a particular wool will work?

I don't always know if a particular piece of wool will work, and I'm not afraid to admit it. What I tell students is to learn your wool. Get a piece of backing fabric, and use it to hook samples of various pieces of wool. The more you hook with textures, the more you begin to understand how they'll look when hooked. Herringbones, houndstooth checks, and big plaids create different looks. Regardless of whether the wool is dyed or as-is, you need to see how the various wool textures change when you hook them. Herringbones look like subtle solids when hooked, whereas plaids take on a characteristic of their own depending on the size and colors in the original plaid. The best way to learn is to take a piece of wool and hook a section measuring about 2" x 2". When testing big plaids, you may need to hook 4" x 4" swatches.

Hooked swatches

"Give it time" is another thing I tell students. Many will hook something and hate it right away. Don't judge a particular wool until you've hooked some other colors around it. It's amazing how colors change when they butt against another color.

I can guide you to a certain point, but when it comes to using color palettes that are substantially different from mine, you need to try it and see how you like the results. There really is no 100% guarantee that your color choices are always going to work. This is a trial-and-error fiber art, but the more you use different textures of wool and the more you settle into your own personal color palette, the more your confidence will grow.

Hooker's Hint: Gaining Experience
- Take a class or two from teachers who have considerable experience. They've made lots of mistakes along the way and are willing to share their experiences and knowledge.
- Go to a rug camp or workshop. Meeting new people who have the same interests as you is fun. It's also very educational to see how other people perceive color and design.
- Join a rug-hooking guild. Attend hook-ins. Go to a rug show. Buy rug-hooking magazines and books. You'll be exposed to a wealth of ideas, tips, and techniques.
- Most of all—have fun!

4. What's your most important tip?

I don't know if there is one tip that is truly more important than another. I have a few that I usually try to stress. These are in no particular order since they are all important.

- Always square up the pattern before you begin hooking (see "Drawing the Pattern" on page 13).
- Be kind to your hands. Match your hook size to the backing fabric you're using, the size cut you're hooking with, and your own comfort zone.
- When you're wool shopping, buy what you like. If you really like it, buy several yards.
- If you're dyeing wool for a project, dye more than you think you'll need. It's always better to have too much than too little.
- Give your rug time to develop before you rip something out.
- Step back from your work and take a good look at the entire piece.

- If you're unhappy with the way your rug is going, put it away for several days and then look at it again.
- Hook what you like and use colors you prefer. Don't feel compelled to do what a teacher tells you to do when you don't agree with him or her. Be confident enough to express what you like.
- It's your rug, your time, and your money—so hook what you like and be happy!

Hooker's Hint: Composition

- If you hook something that you decide you don't like, don't rip it out right away. Give it a chance. The look may change considerably after you've added the background or other surrounding colors of wool.
- Stand back from your work occasionally. What looks good up close may not from far away and vice versa.
- If you're struggling with a rug that just doesn't seem to be working, put it away for a few days, weeks, or even months. When you pull it out later, you might see it all differently.

Hooker's Hint: Dyeing

- Always dye more wool than you think you'll need.
- Try several different brands of dyes and figure out which ones produce the colors you like.
- Practice patience. The dyes you use, the colored wool you are overdyeing, and your water are all variables in dyeing. That said, water is the variable you have the least control over. Not only does the mineral content, acidity level, and chlorine content change from place to place, these variables can change in your home from day to day.

---

5. What's your secret for dyeing wool?

I don't believe I have any deep, dark secrets about wool dyeing. I use lots of formulas from many different dye books. I also use some of my own formulas that I've developed and others that were mistakes that turned out great.

It's not a secret, but I dye over lots of similarly colored pieces of wool. My thinking is that if I start with similar colors but different textures of wool, and then I dye them all with the same formula, they will go together. Some people like the mottled look they get by dyeing large pieces of wool and crowding them into a pot. That technique produces some beautiful wool that hooks up nicely with a unique character of its own. Personally, I prefer using many smaller pieces of wool with different textures but similar colors when I dye.

My favorite wool dyes are those from Cushing. I know that ProChem dyes are more economical, and I use them a lot. But I started dyeing with Cushing dyes and simply know how to manipulate them better. When I spend a day dyeing wool for a workshop, I need to use my time efficiently. I'd rather dye wool once, knowing I'll get the results I want. So I use the formulas I know work for me. When I have time to play in the dye pots, I try lots of different things. Some of the results are great, and some are downright ugly!

There really are no secrets to dyeing. The biggest variables are water, the colored wool you dye over, and the dyes used. The best advice I can give is to do it. Dye often and get to know what works.

DESIGNING RUGS

MANY PEOPLE HAVE asked me how I design my rugs. They want to know what inspires me, and once I'm inspired, how I go from initial idea to final design. With each hooked-rug project in this book, I explain where the idea came from. You'll see some that were influenced by old rugs, some from research done years ago on antique quilts, and some inspired by my love for fall, Halloween, and doodling.

Before I go any further, I need to explain my style. I love all hooked rugs. I marvel at the highly shaded, extremely realistic, fine-cut rugs, but that's not me. They don't fit my home decor or my temperament. I lack the patience and discipline they take. I love primitives. To me, primitive is a style, and the rugs I am drawn to are the old rugs that show design, warmth, and creativity from the soul of the maker.

To me, primitives are simple but heartwarming in design. They are muted, mellow, and rich with faded colors, and they can be made of wool, cotton, silk, yarn, or any combination thereof. They express, enrich, and share a piece of the designer's past. The designers and makers were not trained in the arts. The designs came from within; the designers used what they had to express their talents.

Reading about our ancestors conjures up visions of women hard at work. Yet, among their many daily chores they found time to make simple utilitarian items that added warmth, charm, and color to their homes. Just think

Primitive rugs are most often made from wool, yarn, and cotton.

about it. These were women who rose before sunrise and worked until long after sunset. They had no modern conveniences, no supermarket down the road, no shopping malls, and definitely no take-out food. They did it all—grew the food that fed their family, washed clothes on a washboard, cooked over an open fire, made all the family's clothes and bedding, cared for their children and their home, and still found time to use leftover scraps to create beautiful, functional items that today are sold at auctions for a lot of money.

Just reading that and letting your imagination wander should give you some ideas. With primitive hooked rugs you need to think simple. You need to think about using what you have rather than dyeing everything so that your design is perfectly color planned. So with that in mind, I use a five-step design process that works for me: inspiration for ideas, sketching, refining the design, creating the pattern, and finally color planning. Each of these steps is described below.

Inspiration for Ideas

Many of my inspirations come from reading. I love historical fiction, mostly pertaining to American history. I love books—especially ones with pictures. I love historical places, particularly ones that show how people lived in the past. One of my favorite spots is Colonial Williamsburg. It's always been a favorite of mine, even before I lived only two hours away. Museums that have folk art, textiles, and historical artifacts really interest me.

I can't say precisely when I became interested in historical things, because history sure wasn't my favorite subject when I was in school. In my adult life, I was lucky to have lived in Louisville, Kentucky, for quite a while. I took several classes on the lawn at Locust Grove, the historic home of George Rogers Clark. One of those classes was basket weaving. I loved the Clark house and toured it many times. It was in Louisville that I got involved in quilting. I think those two things jump-started my interest in history.

Now I live in Virginia, and it is just full of history. Thomas Jefferson's gorgeous estate, Monticello, isn't far from where I live. It's incredible. Here is a house built by a man who was way ahead of his time. My favorite time to visit Monticello is the one Saturday a year, just before Christmas, when they have a candle-light tour.

So how does all of this influence or inspire my rug designs? I don't really know how to answer it except to say that I love the allure of that slower, simpler time period. Life back then was incredibly labor-intensive, but it was slower, with no everyday bombardment of horrific news, no commutes to work, no car pools, no rat race in general. While you did your chores or whatever, you had time to let your mind wander and take in the beauty around you.

This is what I did when I designed my first rug, My Old Kentucky Home (see page 27). We were living in a house in the woods where there used to be a Boy Scout camp. On our property we had an old picnic table complete with a leaning cover to protect us from the elements as we dined. We even had a two-seater outhouse that we eventually converted into a storage shed. We had the house designed and built after a trip to Colonial Williamsburg. I wanted a true old-fashioned colonial home. Not only was it a brick colonial, it had a wonderful picket fence and colonial-style self-closing gate with a chain and heavy iron cannonball attached to the gate and fence post.

This home served as inspiration. Take a look at your house. Look at it through the eyes of a child—what do you see? I saw a red brick house, trees (I only included one), a cat because we had four at the time, a rabbit (we had lots of them), the fence I loved, and one of the numerous birdhouses that sheltered many of my friends. That was simple, wasn't it? I now challenge you to design a rug using your house as your inspiration.

Sketching and Refining the Design

I'm a doodler. When I get an idea, I'll scribble it down and play with it. I may try many different versions before it becomes the real thing. Let's look at My Old Kentucky Home rug (the project begins on page 44). The house was the most important item, so I knew I wanted it to be the focal point—the main design element of the rug. A focal point doesn't have to be smack dab in the center, but near there. Next I wanted a tree. Remember: think simple. My tree sort of tells you it's an evergreen and not a deciduous tree. Next came the fence, which I put only on one side because I didn't want to work around the tree. Do you notice that "simple" concept again? The cat seems a little large compared to the house, tree, and fence. One might think it's in the foreground and therefore should be larger. But if the truth were known, I don't hook in little cuts, so the cat had to fit a #8 cut. Also, remember that in primitives, proportions are often quite different than what they are in reality.

Doodles

The size of this rug was to be 36" x 24". I determined the size based on the elements I wanted to include: the house and several other motifs I wanted around the house. I also wanted some kind of border, and the border needed to be large enough for our name to fit. Those were my criteria for this rug.

Now really look at this pattern. There is a focal point, and it is surrounded by other motifs. There are no huge empty spaces. It's not top-, side-, or bottom-heavy. It is pleasingly balanced. Balance is important. It is just as important in the design as it is in your color choices. You want your eye to roam comfortably around the

entire rug. You don't want it to notice one thing and stop.

When designing a rug, give the entire pattern some serious thought. Yet, remember that your design can be changed. Consider the following:

- What is the approximate size I'd like the finished rug to be?
- What is the central focus of the rug?
- Is the focal point in the center or close to the center of the design?
- Will there be other motifs in the rug?
- Do I want a border?
- If so, is this border a simple frame, or does it need to have size and character?
- Is the design balanced?
- Are there any big empty spots?

Perhaps every item on this list won't apply to every rug design, but it's a good starting point when you set out to design your rugs. Askew, on page 50, doesn't exactly follow the above criteria. This rug is balanced in its own way and has a very simple framing border or stopping point. I didn't just keep drawing wiggly lines and circles, and leave it up to your imagination as to when and where it all stopped.

Less Is More

Earlier, I said to keep it simple. By simple I mean clean, not cluttered. When it comes to primitives, less is more! I've seen some fabulous designs lose their importance because there were too many elements jammed into the rug.

A fair guideline is to focus on the approximate size of the rug you're thinking of, the main element of the rug, and whether it needs a border. If you think it needs a border, will the border be wide, narrow, simple, or complex? Is the rug telling a story of some kind? My Old Kentucky Home rug tells a story about where I lived. This rug required more than just the house to tell the story.

When I look critically at this rug, I consider the tree, fence, and path to be elements of the background. They tell part of the story, but they fade away, whereas the cat, rabbit, and birdhouse are more important elements in the story, so they are featured more prominently.

If I were to have shown all four cats, more of the wildlife that frequently visited us, or several more of the birdhouses, this rug would have been so cluttered that it would have lost its story and pleasing nature.

With each rug pattern in this book, I point out how less is more. None of the patterns are complex or cluttered, but some are definitely very simple in design.

Borders

I do not profess to be the authority on borders, but over the years I have seen many rugs. Some of these rugs have had predominant borders, some had none, and some had borders that were very simple. I've seen borders that have taken a good rug and made it great; conversely, I've seen some borders that have ruined an otherwise good rug design.

Each rug is different and therefore dictates whether it needs a border. I'll cite some borders that work and why. In Primitive Posies, shown opposite (pattern is available in *Purely Primitive*), I felt this rug called for a border. The center design was a simple basket of flowers, and the background was rather plain and quiet. A hit-or-miss border was a good way to repeat the colors used in the center of the rug to frame and complement the central design. The border is not heavy or overwhelming, and I didn't introduce any colors that weren't already used in the rug.

Rugs such as Old Homestead, above right, and Antique Pennies, opposite (both patterns are available in *Purely Primitive*); Sun, Moon, and a Few Stars (see page 63); and Bird among the Flowers (see page 72) needed borders but just

Old Homestead hooked rug

Border sketches

simple borders that measured anywhere from 1¼" to 2¼" wide. In contrast, two rather small rugs—My Old Kentucky Home, which is 36" x 24", and Cat Birds, which is 29" x 26"—have borders measuring from 3" to 4¼" wide.

Primitive Posies hooked rug

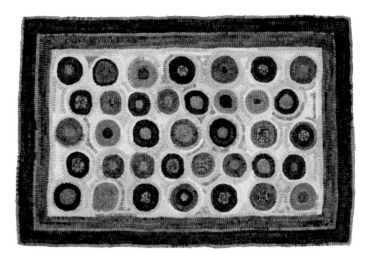

Antique Pennies hooked rug

My Old Kentucky Home hooked rug

Cat Birds hooked rug

I've tried to come up with a rule of thumb regarding rug sizes and how wide the borders should be. But it doesn't work. What I've come to realize over time is that the border needs to be appropriate for the entire rug. Drawing a rug full-scale on paper and looking at it for several days may be your best guide. You just don't want a border that is too heavy or too busy.

Borders that have absolutely nothing to do with the rug design or that introduce colors not shown in the body of the rug almost never work. The border should enhance or frame the rug. It can be as simple as two rows hooked completely around the outside of the rug as I've done on Witch Way on page 55 and Askew on page 50. Or it can be a rather wide 5" border as in Quilted Cats on page 78 and introduce another playful element to the overall design.

All of this information is nothing more than guidelines, things that have worked for me in designing most of my rugs. Some of my favorite antique rugs follow no rules, fit no guidelines, and have no rhyme or reason to them. Maybe that is why I am drawn to them. I don't sit down and check off criteria when designing a rug, and I hope you won't either. This chapter was meant only to give you some insight into what inspires me and how I get from point A to point B in the design process.

Creating the Pattern

I cannot draw—large-scale, that is. I can make small drawings, but to sit down and draw out a pattern for a 36" x 24" rug is something I can't do. Look at my sketch of what eventually became my Bird Dogg rug pattern in *Purely Primitive*. I remember doodling this while sitting in the car waiting for my husband. You'll even notice that I planned the color scheme then too. The final rug design was like the sketch,

dyed black dog & bird
background – gray greens, silo silver,
khaki greens, pieces of red, blue & rust

Small drawing of Bird Dogg hooked rug

but the colors changed a bit. This initial sketch measured about 3" x 2" and the pattern turned out to be 39" x 23".

Quilted CATS by Pat Cross

Grid paper used for designing

So how did I go from a tiny sketch to a big pattern? I played with the enlarger on the photocopy machine at my local copy center. With this pattern, I enlarged the sketch 150%. I enlarged that enlargement another 200% and then another 200% more. That's why I call it *play*. You have to enlarge it in sections, and then tape the sections back together like a puzzle. It may sound like a lot of work, but to me it's play.

When I don't have a final rug design, but I do have lots of shapes or elements that might eventually become a rug pattern, I enlarge them to different sizes for templates. These various templates become my pieces to the rug puzzle, which is how I created Bird among the Flowers on page 72.

Favorite Tools for Designing

I've already told you about the copy machine that enlarges my tiny sketches, but one of my very favorite tools is a huge pad of easel paper that is marked off in a 1" grid pattern and that is often used on flip charts at businesses. You can find this paper at most large office-supply stores. The pads measure 26" x 31" and have faint blue grid lines, perfect for drawing patterns. For larger patterns, I tape pieces together.

I started using this paper a long time ago because of the grid and because it helped me visualize my designs. To me, it's more economical to waste a piece of paper than to draw the pattern on linen and hate it.

Other tools I use are a No. 2 pencil, a soft gum eraser, and a Sharpie permanent marker to draw over my final design when I'm happy with it.

My favorite backing fabric is primitive linen. There are several types of linen available now, but my favorite is the old standard, primitive linen. By using primitive linen and the white grid paper, I can eliminate the need for Red Dot Tracer, netting, screening, or a light box to transfer my designs onto the linen. If I place the light-colored linen on top of the design that has already been outlined with a bold, black line and I have good lighting, I can see the design right through the linen.

Color Planning

Over the years I have taken classes from many great primitive-style rug-hooking teachers. But early on, I remember one of them saying that when it came to color planning, keep it simple. The "rule of three" was mentioned many times. The idea was to use three colors plus a background color for a rug. In each of those three colors, pick three different values: light, medium, and dark.

Of course, back when I started hooking, the fabulous selection of wool we have today wasn't available. Most of our choices were white, off-white, and solid-colored wool. There were some plaids and herringbones, but none of the great textures we have now. Achieving the light, medium, and dark values we needed for primitive rugs meant we had to dye them ourselves. We started with off-white wool and, using the same formula, dyed one-fourth of it light, one-half of it medium, and the remaining one-fourth of it dark. Take a look at the sky in My Old Kentucky Home. At the time, using this method was the only way I could produce the sky I envisioned.

Today with all the fabulous wool available, the sky is the limit. One of my favorite wool suppliers has had wool milled for us. Occasionally an entire page of a flyer might contain several different wool swatches that are totally color coordinated. You can't get much simpler than that.

Even with all this luscious wool, my mind still thinks of the rule of threes. It's a good starting point, especially for new rug hookers or for those that just aren't ready to jump in and use a lot more colors.

Another method I like to use, now that we have so many choices, is to pick a fabulous plaid that I know I want to use. I refer to it as the inspiration piece. Below are three examples. Look at them closely.

The dominant color in swatch 1 is red, but there is also gold, green, and black or deep navy blue. If you were to use this great plaid in a border, I would recommend letting it dictate the colors you use in the center of your rug—reds, greens, and golds of varying shades—and possibly a black background. This is a great example of the rule of threes: red, green, and gold—with a black or navy background.

Swatches 1, 2, and 3

The dominant color in swatch 2 is purple, but this swatch also contains blue. Actually, I see two blues. One is more teal and the other is a lighter blue. There is a hint of red, gold or tan, and a dark shade that appears black, brown, or deep purple, depending on what it's placed next to.

You don't need to use this wool as a border. It would make great flowers with centers that might be red or that golden-tan stripe that's running through the plaid. The purple section might make a great Halloween sky and the blue section looks like cool water to me.

This piece of wool may not seem to fall into the rule of threes, but it does. There is purple (two values—medium and dark), blue (two shades—lighter blue and teal), the red and gold threads, and the dark background (which is either black, brown, or deep purple).

The dominant color in swatch 3 is a wonderful, rusty red. Look at that fabulous pop of blue and the beautiful gold running through it. I've been told that a rug hooker used this as a background, and it was the perfect wool for the rug.

I hope you'll start to look at wool differently. Don't just look at the whole. Look at the parts. These big plaids can be overwhelming, but many of them have incredible sections of color that no amount of overdyeing will give you. They also present great color palettes for those who are uncertain of what colors go well together.

> ### Hooker's Hint: Color
> - Be true to yourself. Use colors that make you happy. Develop your own personal color palette.
> - Be open enough to try something new. You might find you really do like a color that you've never tried before.
> - Natural daylight is the best light for looking at true color.

PUNCHNEEDLE EMBROIDERY— MINIATURE HOOKED RUGS

THE **HISTORY OF PUNCHNEEDLE** is varied. Some sources I've read said it goes back to fifteenth-century Egypt when hollowed-out bones from bird wings were used to punch fibers through a backing.

Other sources cite a Russian heritage. This story dates to the seventeenth century when the Russian Orthodox Church was going through major changes. People not going along with the changes were persecuted, and they scattered to remote areas of Russia and other places around the world. They were known as "Old Believers" and used this type of embroidery to embellish their clothing. Thus, the art form has been referred to as Russian punchneedle.

Another story about the history of punchneedle seems to mimic the history of rug hooking. It says the art form was created by sailors who spent long months at sea and used whatever supplies they could find to create hooked rugs. This theory says that sailors used threads from torn or used sails and a fine, hollow bone of a bird to hook rugs. It all sounds very reasonable to me.

Whichever account is correct, we may never really know. What we do know is that the art form has been around a very long time, and recently it has become very popular. Punchneedle embroidery caught my attention for two reasons. First, it's very portable and, second, it allows me to make miniature hooked rugs.

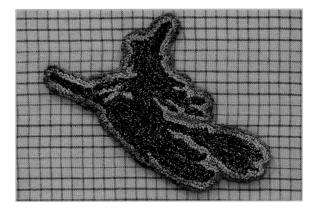

Russian Punchneedle versus Traditional Punchneedle

A very popular form of rug hooking these days is called traditional punchneedle. In this form, you use a heavy-duty punchneedle that has been threaded with yarn, and you punch the rug design from the back of the rug surface. This technique can use strips of wool, as in traditional rug hooking, but it's most often done with yarn.

Russian or miniature punchneedle uses a much smaller and finer hollow needle that is threaded with embroidery floss. To compare the size difference, think how small a #3-cut strip of wool is versus a #10-cut. One is like a thread and the other is like a rope—not exactly, but you get the idea.

Russian punchneedle is a finer, more detailed art form than traditional punchneedle. The principle is the same, but the end result is quite different.

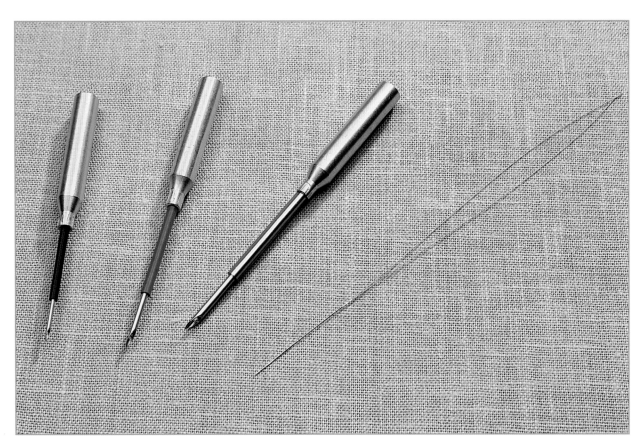

Igolochkoy one-, three-, and six-strand punchneedles with threader

Necessary Equipment

Punchneedle. These come in different needle sizes and handle styles. I used the three-strand Igolochkoy needle for both punchneedle projects in this book.

- A one-strand needle uses only one strand of embroidery floss and produces great detail.
- A three-strand needle can use two or three strands of floss.
- A six-strand needle uses six strands of floss.

Needle threaders. One comes with your needle, but I suggest you purchase extra threaders because they are so easily lost or broken.

Embroidery floss. Standard embroidery floss consists of six strands of thread. One of those six pieces of thread is what I'm referring to when I say a strand.

Samples of punching threads: *left*, cotton floss; *top*, wool floss; *bottom right*, overdyed cotton floss,

- Traditional floss, such as DMC, Anchor, and JP Coats, comes in many colors, is inexpensive, and can be purchased at any craft store.
- Weeks Dye Works floss is hand-dyed. The colors of these fibers vary and give a muted, old look similar to wool that is used in hooked rugs.
- The Gentle Art floss is also hand-dyed. It produces the same effect as the Weeks Dye Works floss but offers other color options.
- Other fibers can be used if they are fine enough to fit through your punching needle. Fine wool threads or flosses work well, as do some pretty ribbons.

Embroidery hoop. Because your backing fabric must be very taut, you'll need a hoop that does not allow your fabric to slip. My patterns are not particularly tiny, so I'd recommend a 7" or 8" hoop.

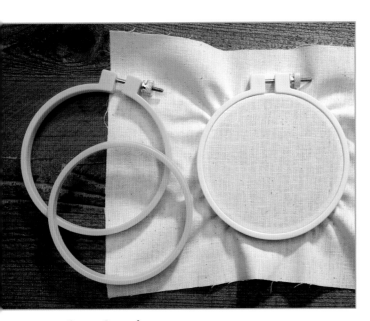

Susan Bates hoops

- Susan Bates locking hoops are very inexpensive and can be purchased at craft and discount stores.
- Morgan Hoops also offers no-slip hoops, including a model on a lap stand. These hoops operate with a tongue-and-groove system to hold your work tautly.

Backing fabric. Any tightly woven fabric can be used. Weaver's cloth is my personal choice. It comes in white, natural, and khaki colors and can be purchased at almost any fabric store.

Backing samples *from left to right*: **natural, white, and khaki weaver's cloth**

Marking pen. Use a very fine-point permanent marking pen, such as a Pigma pen, which can be found in most craft or quilting stores.

Scissors. A small, sharp pair of embroidery scissors is best.

Transferring Your Pattern

There are two simple ways to transfer the pattern. One is by using a light box, and the other is by using a sunny window.

Small light boxes are often available at local craft stores. You can also make a simple light box at home. Any table that opens in the middle for adding extra leaves is perfect. Purchase a piece of Plexiglas or tempered glass and rest it in the opening. Put a lamp without a shade under the opening, and you have a homemade light box.

Because these patterns are so small, if you don't have a light box, it's just as easy to use the window or sliding-glass-door method.

1. Trace the pattern from the book onto any white paper using a fine-point black marker. I usually use paper from my printer.

2. Tape the pattern onto a window that has sunlight shining through it.

3. Tape the piece of weaver's cloth over the pattern. Make sure that the weaver's cloth is centered and that the grain lines are straight.

4. Using your fine-point permanent marking pen, trace the pattern onto the weaver's cloth. If you make a slip or slight error, don't worry. This is the side you'll be working from, which will be the back of the finished piece. Any goofs won't show on your finished work.

Placing the Pattern in the Hoop

Personally, I prefer a 7" hoop for the patterns in this book. I like to center the entire pattern in the hoop and not have to reposition it as I work. Putting the fabric in the hoop really isn't hard, but it always makes me think twice. It's important to use a hoop that has a locking lip on it (such as Susan Bates hoops) to hold the fabric taut. When putting the fabric in the hoop, make sure the part of the hoop with the lip edge is on top of your fabric.

1. With the marked pattern facing up, place the fabric over the inner ring of the hoop.

2. Make sure the pattern is centered, and then carefully slide the larger part of the hoop on top of it.

3. Slowly tighten the hoop, being careful to keep your pattern centered. Before the hoop is completely tightened, stretch the fabric so it is very taut. When you thump a finger on the taut pattern, it should sound like you're hitting a drum. Continue tightening the hoop so that the fabric can't slip.

4. Occasionally, you may have to tighten the fabric as you work. It's much easier to punch when the fabric is very taut.

Threading the Needle

At first, threading the needle may seem tricky, but after you do it a couple of times you'll not give it another thought. The instructions may all seem backward because the process is opposite to almost every other threading process you've done. Don't worry—it works. These directions are for right-handed people. If you're left-handed, simply start by holding the needle in your right hand.

1. Hold the needle in your left hand. Pick up the threader with your right hand and pass it through the hollow, beveled point of the needle. Pass the open or looped end of the threader through first and push the threader through the handle of the needle until the loop end comes out the open end of the handle.

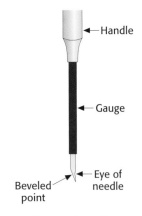

The punchneedle

The threader

Insert the looped end of the threader through the beveled eye of the needle.

2. Cut a length of floss about 24" long, and place it through the looped end of the threader so that about 3" of floss extends through the loop. Tug the floss toward the looped end so that it will stay securely in place during the threading process.

3. Gently grasp the fine, single end of the threader that is still protruding out of the needle shaft to pull the threader completely down and out of the needle.

4. Push the fine end of the threader through the eye of the needle at the beveled end to thread it. Once you've gotten the threader and a few inches of floss through the eye of the needle, remove the thread from the threader. Place the threader in a safe place.

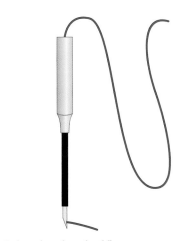

Only a short length of floss extends from the eye of the threaded punchneedle.

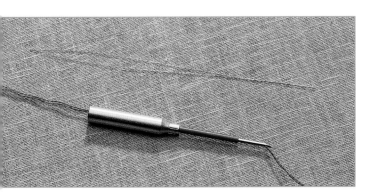

Threaded needle

Before you start punching, make sure you have about an inch of free thread coming out of the eye of the needle and that the rest of the thread coming out of the handle hangs loosely over your hand.

How to Punch

You've made it this far. Now it's time to get punching. I'd suggest you start on a scrap piece of weaver's cloth until you get the feel for using the needle. Draw a wiggly line and follow it. If you need some more practice, draw a heart and outline it. Practice filling in a couple of rows of the heart. With just a little bit of practice you'll be ready to punch your first miniature hooked rug.

1. Hold your needle in a vertical position so that it's perpendicular to the pattern in the hoop. I grasp the needle between my thumb and index finger.

2. With the beveled point of the needle facing the direction you plan to punch, push the needle through the fabric until it stops. The plastic gauge on the shaft of the needle will cause it to stop.

3. Pull the needle up gently. You do not want to pull the needle away from the surface of the fabric. Just pull it out of the fabric and gently drag it (not literally—just a tad off the surface) a few threads forward and punch again. This may feel awkward at first, which is why I said to practice.

4. The sequence is to punch, pull up, slide, punch, pull up, slide, and punch. Once you develop a rhythm, your loops will be even and all of this will make sense.

Above, punching from wrong side of work; *inset,* right side of work

Punching is similar to rug hooking in so many ways. If you pull up too far on your needle, you'll pull out your loops. You don't want to pack your punch loops. Loops in punchneedle need to gently sit next to one another—not be crowded or packed. Packing loops too close together in both rug hooking and punchneedle causes your project to curl, and it may not lay flat once the piece is complete.

Ending and Starting New Threads
If you don't need to change thread colors, keep punching until you run out of floss. All of a sudden you'll realize you're out of floss because

you have empty holes, or the change in the punching sound will alert you that you no longer have floss in the needle. When you do run out of floss, you can simply trim the end close to the backing fabric. You don't have to worry about knotting it or that it will come out of the fabric.

If you need to change colors, and your needle still has quite a bit of floss in it, hold the last loop you made snuggly in place with your finger. Then pull the needle away from the fabric and clip the thread as close to the fabric as possible. Rethread your needle with a new color and continue punching.

Troubleshooting

Don't be alarmed. We all make mistakes and there are usually some pretty simple solutions.

No loops on the finished side?

- Is your needle threaded properly? Check that first.
- Is your floss flowing easily? Make sure it's free to move. If it's caught on the hoop or pinched under your hand, the added tension can result in no loops.

Ugly, uneven loops?

- Are you lifting the needle off the fabric? You want a smooth, even rhythm: punch, lift, slide, and repeat.
- Are you punching all the way down until the gauge hits the fabric?
- Is your needle going straight into the fabric, or have you started to relax the perpendicular position?
- Is the bevel facing in the direction that you are punching, or have you turned your needle?

Wondering if you can rip out and repunch where those ugly loops were? Yes, you can!

- Gently pull the floss out and trim it off. Do not reuse this floss.
- Gently smooth over the weaver's cloth with your fingernail to try and even out the holes made from the old loops.
- Carefully punch over the area using your new, more refined technique.

Finishing Options

In lots of ways, finishing a punchneedle piece is very similar to finishing a hooked rug. Remove the completed piece from your hoop. The backing will be creased from having been in a hoop and will need to be ironed.

I've read of several methods for ironing miniature punched rugs. Some say just press the backing fabric, and some say press the entire piece. What I have done is steam them just as I do a hooked rug, but on a smaller scale.

Place a dry terry cloth towel on the ironing board. Then place the punchneedle piece facedown on the towel. Take a small terry towel that has been wet and rung out, and place it on top of the piece. Apply a dry iron, but do not iron back and forth. Simply place the iron on top of the piece for about 5 to 10 seconds. Lift it and move the iron to any part that wasn't covered with the first steaming. These are such tiny pieces that steaming can usually be done with one application of the iron.

When steaming a rug, both sides get steamed. I don't think these tiny rugs need that much attention. After they have been steamed on the back side, I turn them over and press the exposed backing fabric to remove any creases. Remove all the towels before this final pressing.

Making Pins

Some patterns for punchneedle are so small that they make wonderful little lapel pins.

1. Cut around the punched piece leaving about ¼" of the backing fabric. Apply clear-drying glue to the fabric and fold it to the back of the punched piece. Hold it in place with your fingers for a couple of minutes until it dries.

2. To give the pin some stability, cut a shape slightly smaller than the finished piece out of cardboard or template plastic. Glue that to the back of the punch piece and wait for it to dry.

3. Cut a piece of wool fabric just a tad smaller than the finished piece but a tad larger than the cardboard or plastic you used to stiffen the pin. Sew a bar pin onto the center of the wool, and then glue the wool piece onto the

back of the finished piece. Let it dry and pin it onto your lapel.

Making Miniature Rugs or Hanging Ornaments

Many miniature punchneedle patterns are replicas of old hooked rugs, and they look wonderful in dollhouses. They can also be finished and hung on grapevine wreaths, feather trees, or small tabletop Christmas trees. They also make wonderful additions to the gift wrapping on that special gift for your best hooking buddy.

To make a dollhouse rug or ornament, trim the backing fabric to approximately ¼". Finger-press the excess backing fabric toward the back of the punched piece. Using two strands of floss, whipstitch around the entire outside edge of the miniature rug.

To finish the back of the piece, cut a small piece of cotton homespun slightly larger than the design. Fold under the raw edges and whipstitch it to the back of your miniature rug.

Framing

The options for framing are limited only by your imagination.

Miniature Cat Birds on page 83 was stitched onto a piece of cotton homespun. The goal was to make the homespun look like matting. To do this, trim the backing to within about an inch of the punched piece. Fold the edges of the backing fabric to the back of the piece and appliqué the piece onto the homespun. Use straight pins to hold it in place while you appliqué.

Brunhilda on page 86 presented a challenge. My intention was to punch the witch, then antique the leftover backing fabric (see following for details on antiquing), and frame it just that way. Unfortunately, I wasn't happy with the way the antiquing turned out. To save my work, I trimmed the punched piece, leaving a ¼" seam allowance, and appliquéd it to orange-and-black homespun.

You can also take your finished and pressed piece to a reputable framer, pick out mat board to go with your colors, and have it framed.

Antiquing with Tea

If you want your finished piece to look old, you might try aging it with tea. You can use instant tea or a very strong solution of brewed tea.

I've used two methods: an oven-baked drying technique and ironing. Both give good results.

Oven method. Mix a tea solution using several tea bags and brew a very strong cup of any unflavored tea, or use about ½ cup of hot water to a tablespoon of instant tea. Paint the solution onto the backing fabric extending around your piece. Make sure to get very close to the loops. It's okay to tea stain the punched portion, but I didn't because of the hand-dyed floss that I used. Place the piece on a cookie sheet and bake at 250° for 15 to 20 minutes. Keep an eye on it so that it doesn't burn.

Iron method. Follow the steps above for making the tea and painting it on your piece. Then instead of drying it in the oven, place the piece on an old towel and press it with a dry iron until it has dried. Be careful not to press the loops.

Both methods can be repeated until you achieve the results you want. Just remember to start light and repeat the process as needed if you want it darker. Once it's dark, you can't go back.

N EEDLE FELTING is the process of continually poking a very sharp barbed needle into wool roving. The continual poking of the needle into the roving, whether it's flat or three-dimensional, is done so that the roving fibers become entangled. The flat piece will adhere to the backing and the three-dimensional piece will become a tightly entangled shape.

The process of felting wool dates back to before the ancient Greeks and Romans. The technique of felting wool was used to produce warm, protective material that was then made into clothing.

Needle felting is a process that was originally used to make industrial felt. Large beds of needles moved in and out of loose fibers to make large sheets of felt. By repeatedly moving over the loose fibers, those thin barbed needles caused the loose fibers to become entangled. This method is referred to as dry-needle felting. There is also a process known as wet-needle felting, but this chapter will only cover dry-needle felting.

Needle-Felting Equipment

Needles. Instead of using many needles, we'll be using just one. Felting needles are thin and not uniformly round like a sewing needle. The needle starts out round at the top, but as it narrows toward the very sharp point, it flattens out into a triangular or cone shape with barbs

along each side. The barbs are little notches in the needle. These barbs are what entangle the fibers as you poke the fibers in an up-and-down motion.

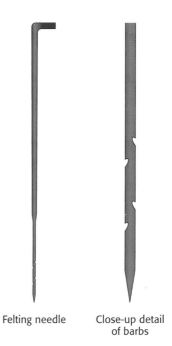

Felting needle   Close-up detail
                        of barbs

Felting needles and foam

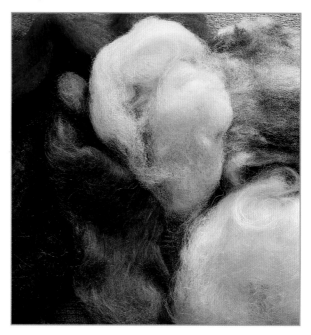

Natural and dyed roving

Needles come in a few different sizes; the higher the gauge, the finer the needle. We will be using the coarsest, 36-gauge needle for dry-needle felting. Since we won't be doing any fine sculpting, it is a good universal needle to use.

Foam. The needle is extremely sharp, so to protect yourself and your work surface you'll need a piece of thick foam. High-density foam sheets can be purchased at most fabric stores. Look for upholstery foam rubber. A piece at least 2" thick and about 12" square is ideal. The overall size of your square can be smaller, but anything less than 2" thick may not protect your tabletop.

If you can't find thick foam, you can also use a large cellulose sponge or a thick piece of Styrofoam. The heavy, gray foam packing material that comes with new electronic equipment is also an option.

Fiber. Wool roving is wool that has been sheared, cleaned, and carded. Sometimes it's referred to as wool fleece. The texture of roving varies from coarse to soft and silky, depending on the breed of sheep it comes from. Coarse is a good general roving to use for the projects

described in this book. Most roving you find will be the kind I've called coarse. Angora roving tends to be softer and silky. If you go to a fiber fair or find a shop that offers both, you'll feel and see the difference. For the projects here, generic roving is what you want.

How to Needle Felt

Two techniques will be covered in this book. One is known as flat needle felting, and the other is three-dimensional needle felting. Regardless of which technique you are doing, you need to hold the needle just below the fattest part of the needle. If you look directly at the needle, it is the widest at the top and tapers down to a fine, thin, sharp point. Hold the needle just below the first tapering between your thumb, index finger, and middle finger.

Rest your arm on your work surface and poke the needle into the wool. These should be short, rapid pokes made by flexing your wrist. This repeated poking motion is what causes the fibers to intertwine and produce a compact mass versus a loose, lofty ball of roving like you started with. This process is called *needling*. The more

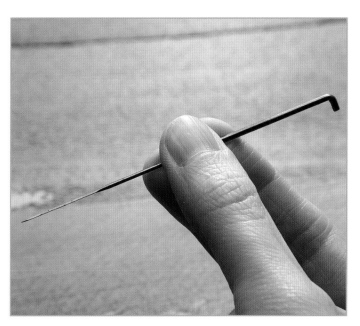

How to hold a felting needle

Flat needle-felting technique

you needle, the denser the wool roving becomes. How tightly compacted your finished product will be depends on your personal preference. You will want to needle long enough so that the fibers are well intertwined and they don't come apart.

Flat Needle Felting

Bird Pillow on page 92 is an example of flat needle felting. With this process, the wool roving is applied or felted onto a piece of wool fabric. To transfer the pattern onto wool fabric, I first drew the pattern onto Red Dot Tracer and then transferred it as I would for a rug-hooking pattern.

1. Place the piece of wool fabric on top of the foam, and then layer small pieces of roving on the wool fabric.

2. Start by outlining on the outside line of the motif with small pieces of roving. You don't want the black line to show, so make sure you cover the line with the roving. If the roving extends way outside the line, you'll end up with a design that is larger than intended.

3. After outlining the entire motif, continue poking the roving until the entire surface of the design area is covered. If there are small details like the ones in the bird, do these and fill in around them with the body color.

4. Occasionally lift the entire piece of wool fabric off of the foam. Because the fibers have been pushed down into the foam a little bit, it will stick, so pull it off slowly. Return the piece to the foam and continue applying the roving until your pattern is completed.

Three-Dimensional Felting

Dimensional needle felting is different from flat needle felting and lots of fun, but it's also the more dangerous technique. The needle is sharp, and because your object isn't lying flat, you'll be more apt to poke yourself. So pay close attention to what you're doing and be careful.

1. To make a ball, take a wad of roving a little bigger than you think you want the finished size to be. Mold it a bit with your hands into a ball shape.

2. Position the foam surface right in front of you, and then lay the ball shape on it and start to poke. As you poke, slowly turn the ball of roving. You goal is to make a compact circle.

3. Keep turning and poking until you like the density and shape of your felted ball.

Pumpkins (see page 90) take a little more detail work. However, they aren't hard when you stop and think about real pumpkins. Most real pumpkins are not perfect in shape. Some are tall and some are squatty, while others have big, flat sides from the way they lay on the ground as they grew.

Safety Tips

- Always work on a foam surface that is large enough for your project. When you're doing flat needle felting, the needle should go no farther than ¼" deep into the foam.

- Keep your needle in one hand and hold the side of your foam with the other. Remember to keep your hands away from the tip and sides of the needle.

- Keep your eyes on the needle as you poke.

- Always know where your needle is. If you pause, stick the needle into the foam. When you've finished, put the needle back into its holder.

- If you are distracted, stop poking!

Three-dimensional needle-felting technique

Samples of four colors of natural-colored roving

Samples of dyed roving

Tidbits about Roving

Roving comes in the natural colors of sheep, ranging from off-white to deep brown. It can be dyed easily. When making three-dimensional items, make the core from natural-colored roving. Finish the item by laying a thin layer of dyed roving over the core and poking it in place. You can purchase dyed roving, but it is more expensive than natural roving.

Dyeing roving is very similar to dyeing wool fabric. If you're only dyeing small amounts of roving, you don't need to fill a big dye pot full of water. The water only needs to be deep enough to cover the roving. When you stir the roving, do it gently. You don't want to tighten or toughen the roving before you use it.

Roving can be found at knitting and weaving stores. It can also be purchased online. The best place to shop for roving is at a fiber festival. Not only will you find all kinds of roving, yarn, and fibers at a fiber festival, but you'll see their source—sheep, llamas, rabbits, and goats. Roving is sold by the ounce and is usually presented in big plastic bags. The bags of dyed roving remind me of bags of cotton candy.

My Old Kentucky Home is the very first rug that I designed myself. I did it at the first rug camp I ever attended at Marion Ham's Quail Hill Workshops in Brunswick, Maine. Part of the program for the week was designing a rug. I don't remember if everyone designed a rug, but I jumped at the chance.

Inspiration

As mentioned earlier, the idea for the rug was to depict my homestead. Since my husband used his woodworking skills to enhance our house and property, my intention was to design and hook this rug to give to him for our twenty-fifth wedding anniversary.

Design Process

This being the first rug I ever designed, I had no process. I was at a workshop, and all I had with me was a small spiral notebook for sketching and taking notes. I doodled from the day we arrived. I knew the basic elements: house, tree, cat, and fence. I also knew the house would be the focal point, but that was it. Drawing a house was easy. This one doesn't really look a great deal like the house in the woods, but it is red brick.

Drawing a tree, on the other hand, wasn't easy. I tried drawing one with lots of limbs, but it looked silly, so I settled on one of our cedar trees. This tree looks more like a simple pine, but you get the tree idea.

Complex and simple tree drawings

As for getting it on paper, that wasn't easy, either. I had lots of little doodles, but no access to an enlarger. Heck, I wouldn't have known about one or how to work one back then. I simply started with the parameters of 36" x 24" and centered the house. Each additional element went in very slowly. The tree filled up a good bit of space. The path was easy, but the fence wasn't. It didn't look good on both sides of the house, so there was a lot of erasing. In the end, there is fence on one side of the house only.

Border

When I finally had this design in the center, it looked lost without a border. At first I drew a border with straight and evenly spaced inside lines. I quickly realized it needed more character, which is when I decided to make the inside edge of the border curved.

Because the border was 3" to 4" wide, I had plenty of room to fill it in with a few hearts, flowers, and our name. Now it looked closer to what I had in mind.

Color Planning

Unfortunately, this rug was not completed for our twenty-fifth anniversary. I had plenty of time to hook it, but I knew in my head how I wanted it to look, and I simply didn't have the right wool or the confidence in my dyeing to create what I wanted. It was five years later when I attempted to produce what I had envisioned.

The givens were a red house with a black roof, a green tree, a blue sky, and some green grass. Actually the roof was hooked with a very dark navy plaid, the same plaid that was used in the border. Although there are several colors used in this rug, the main colors are red, blue, and green. These same colors were repeated in the border motifs.

Materials

Yardages are generously estimated and based on 54"- to 60"-wide wool fabric. Size 8 strips are used throughout this project.

- Backing, 44" x 32" (48" x 36" if using a hoop)
- 1⅓ yards of navy blue plaid wool for border, house roof, and birdhouse roof
- 1 yard of dark red plaid wool for house, flowers, and hearts
- ⅝ yard of shaded soft blue wool for sky and lettering (use darkest value of sky blue for lettering), *or* ⅝ yard of off-white wool for dyeing*
- ½ yard of medium grass-green wool for grass, vines, and leaves
- ⅓ yard of dark green wool for tree, leaves, and vines
- ¼ yard of medium red wool for house foundation, birdhouse, and flowers
- ¼ yard of antique-black wool for cat, front door, and windows
- ⅛ yard of brown plaid wool for rabbit
- ⅛ yard of "dirty" tan textured wool for fence
- ⅛ yard of medium brown wool for tree trunk and birdhouse pole
- ⅛ yard of dark sand wool for path
- ⅛ yard of dull gold wool for bird, windowpanes, and flowers
- 40 yards of navy 3-ply wool yarn for whipping *or* 3½ yards of navy binding tape

*See recipe on page 48 for making dark, medium, and light values of sky-blue wool.

Steps to Make This Rug

1. After enlarging the pattern on page 49 by 400%, transfer it onto the backing of your choice. See "Drawing the Pattern" on page 13 for more details.

2. If you want to put your name on the rug, see "Hooker's Hint: Lettering" on page 48.

My Old Kentucky Home
Finished size: 36" x 24"

3. Outline the roof and fill it in with navy plaid. Follow by outlining the house body and filling it in with dark red wool.

4. Using the same red wool, outline and fill the chimney. Hook the foundation in the medium red wool.

5. Hook the door vertically using antique-black wool. Using the same wool, hook the lines of the windows to outline the windowpanes. Fill the windowpanes with dull gold wool.

6. Hook the tree, cat, rabbit, path, bird, fence, and birdhouse in any order you please. Use the navy plaid for details such as animal eyes and the birdhouse opening.

7. Use the lighter green wool to outline each motif once and then fill in the grass area.

Hooker's Hint: Dye Your Own Sky

If you like to dye wool, here is the recipe I used for making light, medium, and dark shades of sky blue for this rug.

Mix ½ teaspoon of Cushing's Silver Gray with 1 cup of boiling water. Tear ⅝ yard of off-white or natural wool into three pieces: two ⅛-yard pieces and one ⅜-yard piece. Dye as follows:

- Dye ⅛ yard using 1 teaspoon of the dye solution for your lightest value.
- Dye ⅜ yard using 3 teaspoons of the dye solution for your medium value.
- Dye ⅛ yard using 7 teaspoons of the dye solution for your darkest value.

8. Hook the sky horizontally. Start from the grass line and hook about 2" of the lightest sky blue. Continue hooking with the medium sky blue until you're about 2" from the border line. Finish the sky with the darkest sky blue. Remember to gradually change from the lightest value of blue to the medium value, followed by the darkest value. You don't want the transition to be solid horizontal lines, or the sky will look striped.

9. Hook the motifs in the border, including any lettering you've added. Use the red wool for the hearts and flowers, and the dull gold wool for one of the flowers and the remaining flower centers. Use the two greens for the leaves and vines. Fill in the remaining border with the navy plaid wool. Finish your rug according to the directions on page 16.

Hooker's Hint: Lettering

Simple—that was my goal. Knowing I had an area of about 25" x 4" for our last name, I started by printing our last name on scrap paper. The letters had to be less than 4" high so that there would be plenty of room for background. After I got the initial letters looking pretty good, I drew around them to give them width. See the examples. After playing around with their size and shape, I cut them out so I had templates. I positioned the templates in the lower border, centering the O. When I was happy with their placement, I drew around them.

If you feel letter challenged, use your computer. There are many different fonts and sizes. These can be typed out, printed, cut up, and used for templates. If you can't make the size as large as you need, take your printed example to your office-supply store and enlarge it until you get the size that fits. Be sure to keep it simple—a font that has lots of fussy details will be harder to hook.

Write your name.

Outline each letter.

Cut out and use as templates.

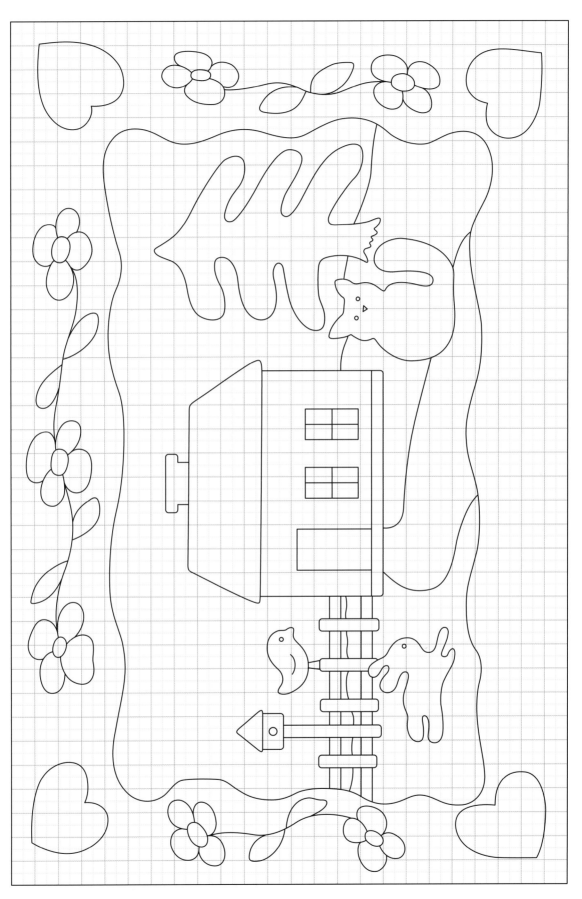

My Old Kentucky Home
Enlarge pattern 400% to 36" x 24".
One square equals ½".

The first time I was scheduled to teach at the Green Mountain Rug School in Vermont, I decided to go a week early and take a class myself. I just wanted to sit, relax, and work on a project that was fun and would hold my attention. I also wanted to work with leftovers. Can you think of anything more indulgent?

Inspiration

Askew is based on an old rug. While I was at a workshop, another participant had a notebook that contained lots of pictures of old rugs. It was there that I saw a small black-and-white photo of part of a rug that featured circles and lines that weren't straight. At the time I thought it was unique, and I sketched some wobbly lines and circles in my notebook.

Design Process

Attempting to draw my interpretation of what was in my notes, I pulled out a piece of primitive-linen rug backing. The size of my linen dictated the size of the rug, and I didn't give much thought to anything other than the size limitation. Using a 3"-diameter circle template, I started drawing circles. Boring! The design needed some help. I pulled out two

smaller circle templates from a box of templates that I keep in my studio and used them to draw inside the 3" circles. For variety, sometimes I used both smaller circles inside the big ones, and sometimes I used just one or the other. To make the rug even more interesting, I drew squares in a few of the 3" circles.

Now it was time for the final touches—those wiggly lines. I didn't measure them or think symmetry; I just drew them. Some are skinny and some are fat. And some are straighter than others. One stripe falls into what you might call the border (one strip-width of black around the outer edge of the entire rug). It's the variation that makes this otherwise simple design interesting. Some of the wiggly lines were tweaked a bit when I was doing the actual hooking.

Border

This rug didn't call for a border, but it did need an ending point. Since one side of the rug had a black edge and the other was khaki, I decided to hook one row of black on the khaki side and on the two short edges too. This framed the rug, but didn't give it a real border.

Color Planning

I knew from the start that I wanted to hook this rug entirely from leftovers so that it would have a scrappy look. Some people think that when I say "leftovers" or "scraps," I mean anything in the "worm" basket—those leftover cut strips. For me, that might work, because my color palette tends to be old and muted. However, I generally don't have a lot of leftover strips because I cut only as I need them.

The average worm basket usually has far too many colors in it. There may be too much contrast or jump in colors and values to use just any leftover strips. The trick to pulling off the sort of scrappy look in this rug is to make sure the colors have subtle contrast. Don't try to use every color of the rainbow.

This rug was hooked using almost entirely as-is wool, including the main colors, black and khaki. The other colors in the rug are reds, teals, greens, purples, and some earthy plaids that contain shots of colors like orange and gold. I did use a little bit of hand-dyed red wool, and the center of one circle contains cotton homespun.

Materials

Yardages are generously estimated and based on 54"- to 60"-wide wool fabric. Size 8 strips are used throughout this project.

- Backing, 44" x 31" (48" x 35" if using a hoop)
- 1¼ yards *total* of khaki textured wool
- 1¼ yards *total* of black textured wool
- 1 yard *total* of red, teal, gold, purple, green, and earthy plaid wool
- Scrap of cotton homespun
- 40 yards *total* of 3-ply wool yarn in 3 to 5 different shades of black for whipping *or* 5¼ yards of black binding tape

Steps to Make This Rug

1. After enlarging the pattern on page 54 by 400%, transfer it onto the backing of your choice. See "Drawing the Pattern" on page 13 for more details.

2. Start hooking one of the circles in the middle of the rug. Start with the outer circle and hook toward the center of the circle, as described on page 15.

3. After you have a few circles hooked, start hooking the wavy-line sections. It might be

Askew
Finished size: 36" x 23"

helpful to mark them *K* for *khaki* and *B* for *black* before you start.

4. After you have worked about three quarters of the center of the rug and are approaching the outside edges, hook one row of black all the way around the perimeter of the rug.

5. Finish your rug according to the directions on page 16.

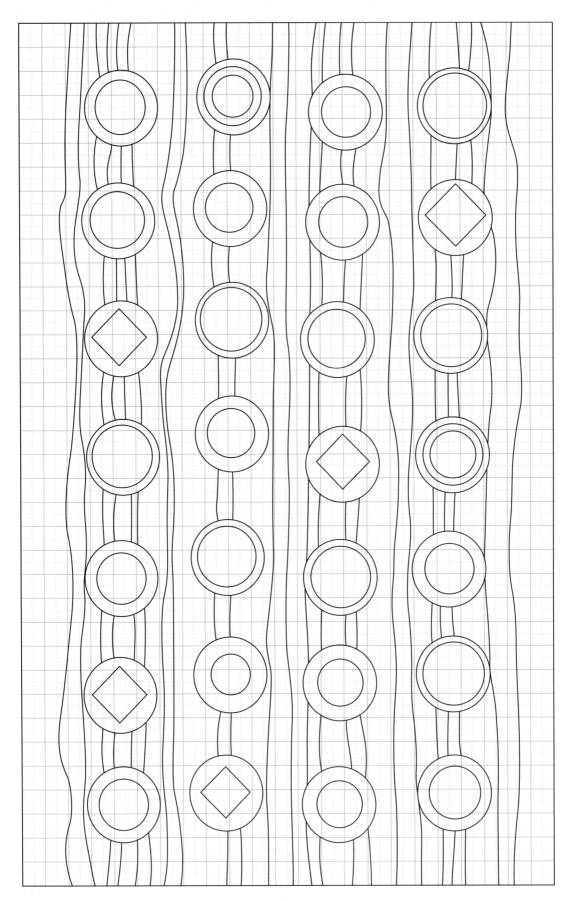

Askew
Enlarge pattern 400% to 36" x 23".
One square equals ½".

Fall is one of my favorite seasons, and I especially love Halloween. I look forward each year to mums, pumpkins, and sweater weather. I live at the foot of the Blue Ridge Mountains in Virginia where the fall color is just incredible. Soon after the school buses start down the road for another school year, I pull out fall decorations and start watching for pumpkins to arrive at the country market.

Inspiration

For years I have kept a folder that contains articles, stories, and pictures about Halloween, fall decorations, and gorgeous scenery. The idea for Witch Way was in that folder. I took the flying witch, a crescent moon, and pumpkin designs from various sources, all of which I had stashed in that folder, and traced them. The pumpkin came from a photograph of pumpkins, the moon came from a card, and the witch was inspired by a witch I saw in a book.

Design Process

I took the sketches of the witch, moon, and pumpkin to my office-supply center and enlarged them to various sizes. Then I cut out the shapes and moved the assorted templates around on white grid paper until I found a pleasing arrangement.

Because the witch was going to be the focal point, I positioned her in the center. Then, I placed the pumpkin and moon so that the design was well balanced and there were no huge blank spaces. Finally, I added a few personal touches to enhance the Halloween design, yet kept it simple and uncluttered. The word *BOO* and a few varying shapes were added to spice up what could have otherwise become a very boring background.

Border

The witch on her broom was what I wanted center stage. The additional elements complemented her. A border of any kind probably would have drawn attention elsewhere, so just a simple frame of two rows of black loops finished this rug.

Color Planning

An orange pumpkin, a golden moon, and a witch with a purple wart on her nose was not what I had in mind when designing this rug. I envisioned mellow touches of Halloween. Since the witch, moon, and pumpkin were the largest elements, I decided they should all be the same color—black, like a spooky Halloween sky. Then I went in search of a background color. I found a great as-is plaid that was perfect for the rug design. It was the combination of orange, lime green, and gold shades in the plaid that made me choose those colors as accents for the rug.

The black was my usual antique-black formula. I overdyed several different wool pieces, so the shades and textures of the black vary greatly. The orange, lime green, and gold were dyed using the Spiced Pumpkin, Lemon Grass, and Broom Straw formulas from the book *Vermont Folk Rugs: Dyeing to Get Primitive Colors on Wool* by Laurilyn Wiles.

Materials

Yardages are generously estimated and based on 54"- to 60"-wide wool fabric. Size 8 strips are used throughout this project.

- Backing, 36" x 28" (40" x 32" if using a hoop)
- 1¼ yards of antique-black wool for witch, pumpkin, moon, and outlining
- 1¼ yards of plaid wool for background
- ¼ yard of orange wool for outlining, letter, and background shapes
- ¼ yard of lime green wool for outlining, letter, and background shapes
- ¼ yard of gold wool for outlining and letter
- 32 yards of 3-ply antique-black wool yarn for whipping *or* 3 yards of black binding tape

Witch Way
Finished size: 28" x 20"

Steps to Make This Rug

1. After enlarging the pattern on page 58 by 300%, transfer it onto the backing of your choice. See "Drawing the Pattern" on page 13 for more details.

2. Hook the witch, moon, and pumpkin using the various shades of antique-black wool. Outline the witch in lime green, the moon in gold, and the pumpkin in orange. Use the same colors for the facial features on the motifs.

3. Hook the word *BOO* in orange, lime green, and gold. Outline the letters with two rows of antique-black wool.

4. Refer to the photograph for the color placement of the various background shapes.

Then hook the background with plaid wool and finish with two rows of antique black around the outer edge.

5. Finish your rug according to the directions on page 16.

Background fabric for Halloween rug

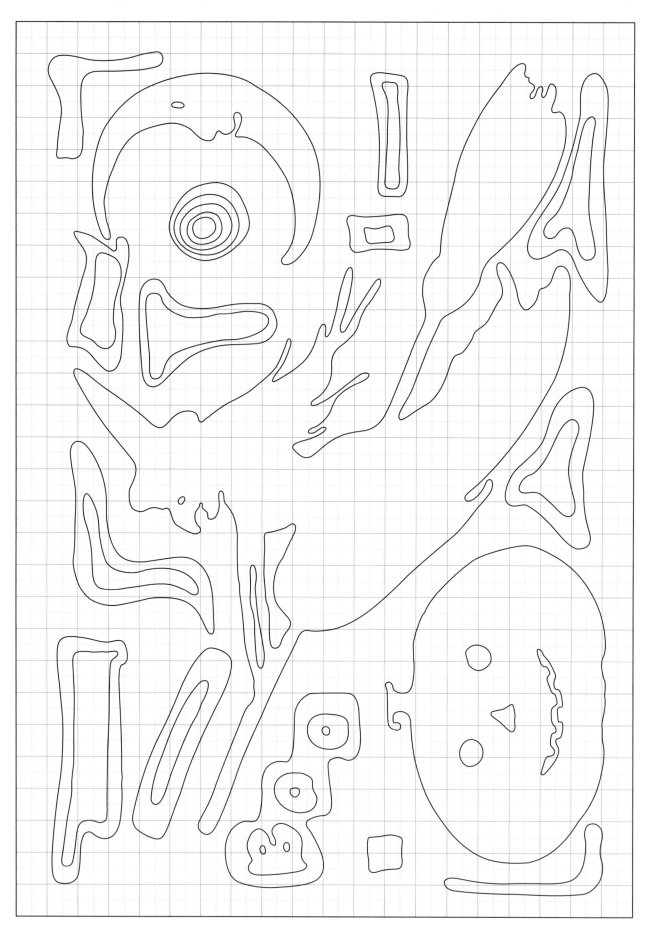

Witch Way
Enlarge pattern 300% to 28" x 20".
One square equals ½".

CAT BIRDS

It was such fun to hook this rug; I enjoyed the challenge of using only two colors of as-is wool. In fact, this was one project that I didn't want to end!

Inspiration

Several years ago I was visiting a friend, and she took me to her mother's house to show me something. While there, we came across a stack of old magazines about decorating and antiques. We took the magazines back to her house and rummaged through them. In the April 1983 issue of the *Magazine Antiques*, I found an ad for American antiques and quilts that captured my attention.

Pictured in the ad was a bedroom filled with several pieces of furniture in a timeworn robin's egg blue color. A wonderful blue-and-white quilt was displayed on the bed. A "Tailor" sign hung over the bed, an embroidered quilt decorated one wall, two beautiful woven rugs lay on the floor, and a stack of pantry boxes sat in the far corner of the room. When I looked closely at those pantry boxes, I noticed a hooked rug hanging on the wall behind them. It was partially blocked from view by several hanging baskets, but I saw enough to fall in love with that rug, and I knew I had to hook one very similar to it.

Design Process

I made a colored copy of the magazine page, but it was difficult to get the gist of the entire rug because it measured only about ¾" square in the picture. Still, there was enough there for me to work up my own interpretation of this antique rug.

I decided to limit the rug to the size of the flip-chart grid paper I use for designing rugs. Thus, Cat Birds became 29" by 26".

Border

The antique rug had a border, and I knew my version needed one very similar to the original. After playing around with the proportions, I decided to make the border 4" wide.

Color Planning

The rug appeared to be done primarily in black or dark brown, and khaki. I love the simplicity of two-colored rugs, so color planning my rug required no serious thought. The trick was to do it entirely in as-is textures. My adaptation of this antique rug was hooked using 11 different as-is black wool textures and seven different as-is khaki wool textures. One khaki texture had two usable sides, and another khaki was also used as a black because it was a tiny black-and-khaki check. Counting these additional versions of khaki, I used nine different as-is khaki textures.

Materials

Yardages are generously estimated and based on 54"- to 60"-wide wool fabric. Size 8 strips are used throughout this project.

- Backing, 37" x 34" (41" x 38" if using a hoop)
- 1½ yards *total* of textured khaki wool
- 1 yard *total* of textured black wool
- 35 yards of 3-ply wool yarn in at least 3 shades to complement black wool used *or* 3¼ yards black binding tape

> **Hooker's Hint:**
> **How to Get the Scrappy Look**
> The best way I have found to get the scrappy look, without unduly stressing over it, is to run each piece of your different blacks through the cutter once or twice to give you a nice mix of the different shades and textures. From this bunch of strips, randomly pick one strip and hook. Then pull another strip from the bunch and hook with it; don't think, just randomly pick one. When you've hooked all your cut strips, cut another batch from each wool and continue hooking.

Cat Birds
Finished size: 29" x 26"

Swatches of fabrics used in Cat Birds

Steps to Make This Rug

1. After enlarging the pattern on page 62 by 400%, transfer it onto the backing of your choice following the instructions on page 13.

2. Hook the wings and facial features in black wool. Outline and fill the cat and birds with khaki wool.

3. Hook the inside border line with black wool and then fill in the background around the birds and cat with the black wool.

4. Hook the scallops, random lines, and flower outlines in black. Cut a strip of black wool in half lengthwise and use it to hook around the bird tail that extends into the border. This will give the tail a gentle highlight and prevent it from getting lost in the khaki border.

5. Hook one row of black along the outside edge of the rug and then fill in the rest of the border with khaki.

6. Finish your rug according to the directions on page 16.

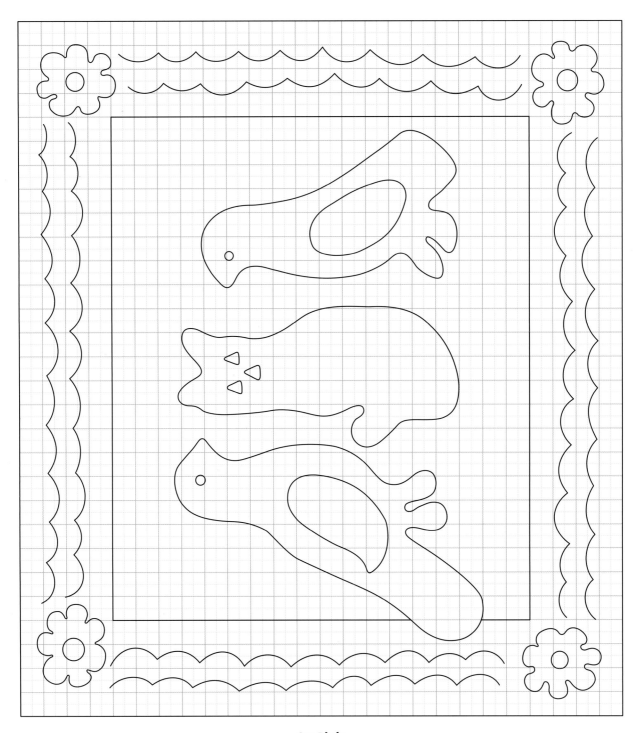

Cat Birds
Enlarge pattern 400% to 29" x 26".
One square equals ½".

Geometrics can be fun, challenging, and boring to hook. The boring aspect stems from hooking repetitive shapes. You can avoid this by adding elements that don't fit into the world of square, rectangular, triangular, or circular. If I had eliminated the sun, moon, and stars from this rug, the result would have been pleasing, but these elements add some whimsy without being cute, and make the design more interesting to look at and to hook.

Inspiration

Several years ago I took a geometric design class at the Green Mountain Rug School in Vermont. I went to class with several sketches on graph paper, but no pattern on my rug-backing fabric. After listening to our teacher, Marjorie Judson from Prince Edward Island, Canada, I designed this rug. Marjorie pointed out how hooking the same shape over and over again could become boring. She wasn't trying to discourage us; she was just pointing out a fact.

However, I liked the idea of simple squares drawn on point, or on the diagonal, but decided to add something to break up the monotony. That's where the stars came from. The stars inspired the moon, and night needed day, thus the sun.

Design Process

I started my design with two dictates in mind. First, I had two different-sized pieces of blank linen with me in class. The rug had to fit on one of them. Second, I liked the idea of making the blocks 2½". It's a nice size to hook when using #8 strips.

A simple pad of ¼" graph paper is a wonderful tool when it comes to plotting a geometric design. I started to draw little 2½" boxes on my graph paper. As I was drawing, I decided that six full blocks running horizontally fit nicely on the size of my linen. I wanted to make the rug rectangular, and I liked the way five blocks high looked with six blocks wide.

To complete the design, I placed the sun rising in the top center as the moon was setting in the lower-left corner. The stars are placed randomly. I prefer odd numbers, so I used five stars to fill out the rug without making it look sparse or crowded.

Border

This rug needed a border, but nothing busy. While it seemed to call for a simple border, I wanted more than just a couple of rows of hooking to frame it. I drew a 2"-wide border around the central design and decided to give the border design great thought as I hooked the main part of the rug.

Color Planning

Less is more, but this rug also called for that little bit of whimsy. Immediately I envisioned the squares as red and black. (Actually, they are Jessie's Apple Red from *Antique Colors for Primitive Rugs* by Emma Lou Lais and Barbara Carroll, and Cinnamon Stick from *Vermont Folk Rugs: Dyeing to Get Primitive Colors on Wool* by Laurilyn Wiles.) The whimsy came from a golden sun and blue moon. And, if you look closely, you will see one tiny strip of lime green used in the sun's eye!

Materials

Yardages are generously estimated and based on 54"- to 60"-wide wool fabric.

- Backing, 36" x 32" (40" x 36" if using a hoop)
- 1¼ yards *total* of black wool for squares, sun's features, and border
- 1 yard of red wool for squares, small star, and border
- ¾ yards of golden yellow wool for sun, large stars, moon's eye and background, grid outlines, and inner-border line
- ⅝ yard of blue wool for moon, sun's eye and background, large star backgrounds, and border
- 40 yards of 3-ply wool yarn to complement black wool for whipping *or* 3¼ yards of black binding tape

Sun, Moon, and a Few Stars
Finished size: 28" x 24"

Steps to Make This Rug

1. After enlarging the pattern on page 67 by 400%, transfer it onto the backing of your choice. See "Drawing the Pattern" on page 13 for more details.

   NOTE: The yellow outlines for the squares and the inner-border line are hooked with #5 strips. The rest of the rug is hooked using #8 strips.

2. Hook all the yellow outlines first, including the inner-border line, to define the squares and edge triangles.

3. Fill in the squares and triangles with the red or black wool. You may find it handy to mark each square and edge triangle with an *R* for red or a *B* for black before beginning to hook.

4. For the solid-colored squares, start hooking around the perimeter of each block, and then hook toward the center following the shape of the block.

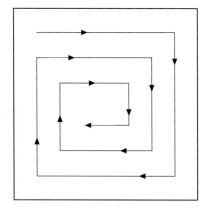

Hooking direction for the squares

5. For the sun block, hook the sun after hooking the eye and other facial features. Follow by hooking the blue background.

6. For the moon block, hook the eye and star; then hook the moon in blue. Finish by filling in the rest of the square with yellow wool.

7. The five large stars are hooked in yellow with blue backgrounds.

8. Hook the border starting from the inside and moving outward. Follow the yellow border line with two rows hooked in blue, and then two rows hooked in red, and end with three rows hooked in black.

9. Finish your rug according to the directions on page 16.

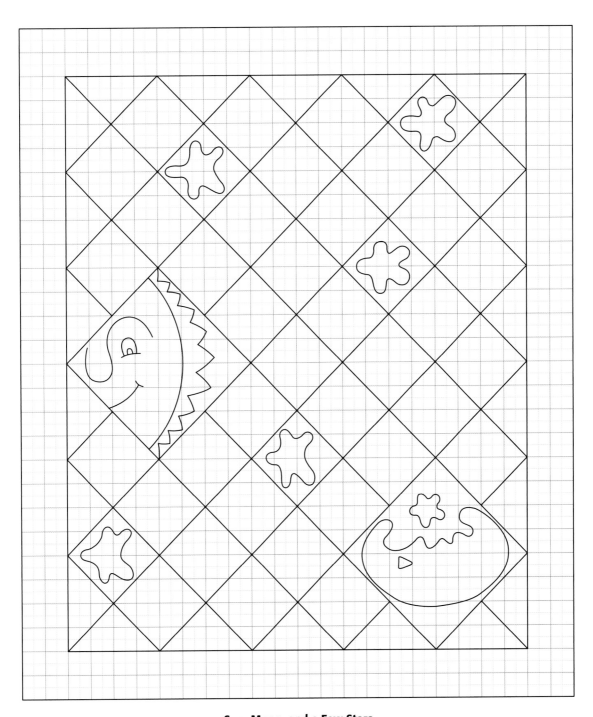

Sun, Moon, and a Few Stars
Enlarge pattern 400% to 28" x 24".
One square equals ½".

Spud—doesn't that name fit him? This design is an adaptation of an antique rug. My notes and scribbles tell me that the original was made in Pennsylvania around 1880. The scrappy manner in which it was hooked is what drew me to it.

Inspiration

The dog was center stage in the original rug, but I remember him being surrounded by birds—bluebirds, if I remember correctly. I loved the simplicity of the dog. And I liked that he was featured prominently, which leads me to believe he was a very special member of the maker's family.

Because that old rug spoke to me, I decided I had to do a similar rendition. I kept the center basically the same, but I encircled Spud with rabbits. He didn't strike me as a real hunter so I could see a big lazy dog just lying under a tree while rabbits ran circles around him.

Design Process

The original rug was 40" by 30". I didn't want to hook a rug quite that large, so I drew my little sketch of the dog and enlarged it several times. When I found a size that made me happy, I put him on grid paper and added a border. I made a tin template of a rabbit and traced around it in all four corners.

Border

The border of this rug is the outer red area where the rabbits run. It frames the oval center where Spud stands. The two simple rows of black around the outside edge frame the entire rug.

Color Planning

This was another fun and simple rug for me. I wanted it to be scrappy, yet somewhat planned. My notes reminded me that a lot of cream, khaki, black, and blue wool was used in the original rug. But, I wanted some pizzazz. I love red, and this rug called for some spark. Therefore I decided the border area outside the dog's oval was to be red. Not just a single red, but lots of reds. Some of the red wool was overdyed, some was as is, and some were plaids that had red as the predominant color.

Materials

Yardages are generously estimated and based on 54"- to 60"-wide wool fabric. Size 8 strips are used throughout this project.

- Backing, 41" x 36" (45" x 40" if using a hoop)
- 1½ yards *total* of textured red wool for flowers, arch, and background frame
- 1⅓ yards *total* of textured khaki wool for center oval and rabbits; use darkest ones for rabbits
- 1 yard *total* of black textured wool for dog, rectangle, and rug perimeter
- 55 yards *total* of 3-ply wool yarn in 3 to 5 assorted blacks for whipping *or* 4½ yards of black binding tape

Steps to Make This Rug

1. After enlarging the pattern, opposite, by 400%, transfer it onto the backing of your choice. See "Drawing the Pattern" on page 13 for more details.

2. Hook the dog using a mix of all your black wool. Hook the rectangle below him in the same manner.

Spud
Finished size: 33" x 27"

3. Hook the lollipop flowers and stems, as well as the small arch over the dog, with red wool.

4. Outline the edge of the center oval using any of your khaki wool. Fill in the entire oval area, randomly mixing the khaki wool.

5. Hook the rabbits using the darker khaki wool.

6. Hook two rows of black around the entire perimeter of the rug. Fill in the rest of the rug with your red textured wool. Note how the hooking direction changes on each side of the rug. This change of direction adds interest to the red frame.

7. Finish your rug according to the directions on page 16.

Spud
Enlarge pattern 400% to 33" x 27".
One square equals ½".

I normally don't hook flowers, and lots of people kid me about that. In fact, a friend saw a preview of my book *Purely Primitive* online and decided I couldn't have written it, because I don't do flowers. Surprise— I do hook flowers. I just happen to prefer animals. This rug evolved from a few tiny sketches of flowers I doodled one day while talking on the phone.

Inspiration

Even though I'm best known for rug hooking, I am still consumed by my interest in quilts, books on quilt history, and antique quilts. I subscribe to a couple of national quilting publications, go to quilt shows that fit my schedule, and seek old quilts and books on quilts whenever I visit an antique shop or bookstore.

This rug was influenced by my interest in quilts. I wanted to hook flowers but didn't want to do a basket of flowers or just run flowers all over a rug. I wanted my flowers to look important, so I decided to play around with the idea of hooking a sampler flower "quilt."

Design Process

Once I seriously looked at my sketches and doodles of a rug layout, I did a little math. The goal was to find a pleasing arrangement and not make a rug that was so big that it could become boring. Through this process I decided that 12" blocks were a good size to feature the flowers, and I preferred that the blocks be turned on point as they are in many appliqué quilts.

My first idea was to use the four outer blocks for the flowers and the center block for a heart or bird. Once I enlarged my sketches to fit 12" blocks, I discovered that the silly little bird fit perfectly in the center. However, at that size I didn't like two of my flower blocks, so I edited them out and simply repeated the two best designs.

Once I had everything drawn to scale, I really began to like the rug and couldn't wait to get started. My mind was going crazy with color ideas.

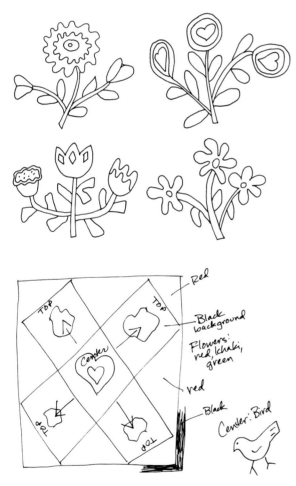

Sketches of flowers and overall layout of "Bird among the Flowers" hooked rug

Border

This rug could have easily grown way too large by the addition of several borders. If you're familiar with quilts, you can see that this rug would make a wonderful center for a medallion quilt. Someday, I may very well expand it. My thinking at the time was to keep it simple.

To keep it simple, I knew I wanted a 1" border, but four rows of one color wasn't the answer. Because I framed the center block with one row of red, I decided the outer border needed one row of a color to separate the rug from the frame.

Color Planning

Hooking flowers opened the possibility of using lots of color, but I like to keep things simple, uncluttered, and red! At the time, I had a few wonderful as-is plaid pieces of wool that contained red, green, and flashes of yellow. There's a decorating program on TV that talks about starting with an "inspiration piece." That plaid wool was my inspiration piece.

With the flowers planned, the question was how to put the rug together so that the elements would be related yet show off each individual block of flowers. Neutrals were the answer—I love neutrals. Khaki, black, brown, gray, and the like are all neutrals in my book. For this rug, the winners were black and khaki.

Although I love black and red together, I knew if I hooked the backgrounds of each "quilt block" in black, the flowers and bird would be lost. So I decided to halo each of them in a simple as-is khaki herringbone. After I hooked the halo, I filled in the remainder of the block with hand-dyed antique-black wool.

From there, the rest of the color choices all fell into place. I knew the outside triangles had to be red. The pencil-line border left me thinking for a while. My first inclination was to use gold, but there really was so little gold in the rug. When I laid a strip of khaki wool between the red and black, it won hands down!

Bird among the Flowers
Finished size: 36" x 36"

Materials

Yardages are generously estimated and based on 54"- to 60"- wide wool fabric. Size 8 strips are used throughout this project.

- Backing, 44" x 44" (48" x 48" if using a hoop)
- 1¾ yards *total* of antique-black wool for block backgrounds, bird's feet, and border
- 1¼ yards *total* of red wool for outside triangles, center block outline, bird, and flowers

- ¾ yards of khaki wool for border line and halos surrounding flowers and bird
- ¼ yard *total* of as-is red plaid wool for flower petals and buds
- ¼ yards *total* of green wool for leaves and stems
- ⅛ yard of gold wool for flower centers
- 55 yards of 3-ply antique-black wool yarn for whipping *or* 4½ yards of black binding tape

Steps to Make This Rug

1. After enlarging the pattern, opposite, by 500%, transfer it onto the backing of your choice. See "Drawing the Pattern" on page 13 for more details.

2. Hook the bird in red wool. Use one of your darker shades of red to highlight his wing and tail feathers. Hook his black feet, and then hook his halo in khaki wool.

3. Outline the bird block with one row of red wool, hooking on the diagonal lines. Fill in the block with antique-black wool.

4. Hook the flower block by starting with the flower centers, and then hook the petals. Hook the stems, leaves, and buds. Then hook the halo behind the flowers and fill in the rest of the block in the same manner as you did the bird. After hooking the khaki halos, it will be helpful to hook the inner-border line in khaki. That way, when you're ready to hook the black backgrounds, you won't inadvertently hook the black across that narrow line.

5. Hook each of the black block edges exactly on the line. Hooking on the line keeps the blocks square. If you venture off the line, the 12" blocks will become larger or smaller, thus messing up the alignment.

6. Hook the red triangles in your manner of choice. I hooked one of them in a triangular fashion, following the outline and filling in with concentric triangles, but I didn't like the way it looked. Personally, I prefer my meandering style, but any way works.

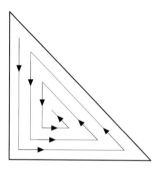

Triangular hooking

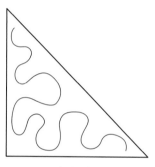

Meandering hooking

7. If you haven't already done so, hook the khaki border line. Then hook three rows using antique-black wool to complete the rug.

8. Finish your rug according to the directions on page 16.

Bird among the Flowers
Enlarge pattern 400% and then 125%
(500% total) to 36" x 36".
One square equals ½".

This rug holds a very special place in my heart. It makes me smile whenever I look at it. I can't explain the reason exactly, but I think it has to do with the memories of a wonderful New England vacation associated with this rug. During a visit to the Shelburne Museum in Vermont in the early 1990s, I spied a wonderful appliquéd album quilt. I wasn't interested in appliqué, but the quilt took my breath away. This rug is based on one of the blocks in that extraordinary quilt, the "Klute Cottage Album," circa 1840–1850.

Inspiration

Since I wasn't allowed to take photographs at the museum, I knew that I had to see my inspiration quilt again. I made arrangements for a personal viewing of the quilt and scheduled a return visit to Shelburne. The blocks in the quilt depict whimsical flowers, cats, birds, and what I assume was the maker's house. (Upon close inspection of the quilt, I discovered that while the quilt is documented as the "Klute Cottage Quilt," the maker's name is actually spelled with a *C*, not a *K*. "E Clute" is very clearly inked on the front door of the house block!)

This time the museum let me take pictures, and my intention was to appliqué the one cat block I loved so much. However, years later at a rug-hooking retreat, I decided that since I had never appliquéd my cat block, I might as well hook it.

Design Process

Initially, when my intentions were to appliqué this design, I traced the block from the photo I had taken. The block was teeny tiny. Without access to a copy machine, I increased the design using ¼" graph paper until I had a block about 12" square. When I changed my mind and decided to hook the design, I enlarged that 12" square to about 24" x 30".

Border

I knew this rug needed a border, but the sashing on the quilt wasn't exciting and didn't seem to fit the rug. To give the frolicking cats a fitting, playful border, I carried the center vine and berry motifs into the border, and added some rabbits. My biggest challenge was determining the border width. I drew one rabbit and a small section of vine with a few leaves and berries. I enlarged my border idea to several different sizes so it would fit a border anywhere from 2" to 6" wide. After deciding that a 5" border looked best, I drew the vine completely around the rug and then played with positioning the leaves, berries, and rabbits.

Color Planning

This rug design had enough activity, so when it came to color I felt that simple was best. I never hook cats in my rugs that depict our pets—past or present. I just can't show favoritism. Since I had decided the rabbits were going to look like the grayish brown ones that ate my pansies, the cats would be the same color.

The inner background color is Corn Silk from *Vermont Folk Rugs: Dyeing to Get Primitive Colors on Wool* by Laurilyn Wiles. The outer-border background is the same color, but I increased the formula to 1½ times the amounts called for in the recipe. A simple, red inner-border line separates the two values. The vines and leaves are Silo Silver, from the same dye-recipe book. The red is Jessie's Apple Red from *Antique Colors for Primitive Rugs* by Emma Lou

Lais and Barbara Carroll. The bluebird and several berries carry blue accents throughout the rest of the rug.

Materials

Yardages are generously estimated and based on 54"- to 60"-wide wool fabric. Size 8 strips are used throughout this project.

- Backing, 46" x 50" (50" x 54" if using a hoop)
- 2 yards of khaki wool for inside background
- 1½ yards of darker khaki wool for the border background
- 1¼ yards *total* of assorted grayish brown wool for cats and rabbits
- 1¼ yards of mossy-green wool for stems, vines, and leaves
- ½ yard of red wool for berries and inner-border line
- ⅓ yard of blue wool for bird, berries, and cats' eyes
- 60 yards *total* of 3-ply wool yarn to complement outer border for whipping *or* 4¾ yards of khaki binding tape

Steps to Make This Rug

1. After enlarging the pattern on page 82 by 600% total, transfer it onto the backing of your choice. See "Drawing the Pattern" on page 13 for more details.

2. Hook one of the cats first. After completing the cat, hook one row of background around him.

3. To keep things interesting, start on the stems, leaves, and a few berries. Then move on to the next cat. The cats are big and can get boring, so vary the sequence of the shapes and colors you hook. Remember to hook at least one row of background around each motif after you hook it.

Quilted Cats
Finished size: 38" x 42"

4. Hook the background behind the cats and finish the area with one row of red to separate the rug background from the border.

5. Hook each section of the outside border as you come to it. By hooking some of the vine, leaves, berries, and rabbits, and filling in the background before you move on, the hooking will be more interesting, and you won't have to go back and fill in background later.

6. Finish your rug according to the directions on page 16.

Molly Nye Tobey

If you live in New England or plan to visit the area, be sure to treat yourself to a trip to the Shelburne Museum in Shelburne, Vermont. During my first visit, I made a beeline to the textile building to see the quilts, which was when I discovered the album quilt with the wonderful cat block. I had no idea that all the Molly Nye Tobey rugs would also be on display.

Molly was born in 1893 in New Bedford, Massachusetts. She learned to rug hook at the age of 14. She graduated from the Rhode Island School of Design in 1915 and from the all-male New Bedford Textile School in 1917. She lived for 91 years, and designing, selling, and teaching rug hooking filled a great part of her life. She is known for designing and hooking one rug for every one of the 50 United States.

All of her state rugs and a nice history of her life can be found in *Hooked Rug Treasury* by Jessie A. Turbayne (Schiffer Publishing, 1997). There is also an article in the September/ October 2005 issue of *Rug Hooking* magazine about the Molly Nye Tobey rugs.

Quilted Cats
Enlarge pattern 400% and then 150%
(600% total) to 38" x 42".
One square equals ½".

MINIATURE CAT BIRDS

This is a replica of the hooked rug Cat Birds. I tried to mimic the rug by using a wide variety of khaki and black threads just as I did with the wool used for hooking the rug.

Materials

- 12" square of natural weaver's cloth
- 1 skein *each* of Weeks Dye Works floss in Rum Raisin, Caper, Molasses, Onyx, Swamp Water, Mascara, Charcoal, Putty, and Palomino
- 2 skeins *each* of Gentle Art floss in Harvest Basket, Tarnished Gold, and Flax
- 1 skein of Gentle Art floss in Dark Chocolate
- Pigma Micron 03 black pen or very fine-point black permanent marker
- 13" x 19" piece of homespun for matting (optional)
- ¼"-thick foam core for mounting (optional)
- 9¼" x 10" frame (optional)★

★The frame shown was made by my husband, Tom Cross. The inside opening is 6¼" x 7", and the outside dimensions are 9¼" x 10".

Drawing the Pattern

1. Photocopy or trace the pattern, opposite. Note that the pattern is the reverse of the project photograph because you'll be punching from the back side. The finished design will be facing the same way as in the photograph.

2. Tape the pattern to a sunny window, and then tape the 12" square of weaver's cloth over the paper pattern. Make sure the weaver's cloth is centered over the pattern and on the straight of the grain.

3. Using the Pigma pen, trace the pattern onto the fabric.

Punching Order

To achieve the variegated blacks and khakis in my punching, I made up a new three-strand variety of flosses each time I threaded my needle. I took one strand each of three different black threads to make this new variety. I repeated this with the khaki threads too. This mimics the use of many different as-is wool shades used in the hooked rug.

1. For the bird eyes, use two strands of black floss in the needle and punch two loops for each eye.

2. Outline and fill a bird using the khaki flosses. Outline the wing and fill it in using the black flosses. Continue with the other bird and cat.

3. Using black flosses, outline the background behind the birds and cat and fill it in. Punch one row around the tail of the bird whose tail overlaps into the border.

4. Using black flosses, punch one row around the entire outside border. Punch the corner flowers and wavy lines. Fill in the rest of the border with khaki flosses.

5. Finish and frame the piece, referring to "Finishing Options" on page 37.

Finished size: 5⅛" x 4"

Miniature Cat Birds pattern

Halloween is spelled *F-U-N* in my dictionary. I love everything about it—fall colors, pumpkins, bittersweet, Indian corn, and kids dressed up in scary costumes! This little witch can be as friendly or as evil as you want her to be.

Finished size: 4¾" x 3½"

Materials

- 12" square of natural weaver's cloth
- 1 skein *each* of Gentle Art floss in Black Crow (black) and Tin Bucket (gunmetal gray)
- 1 skein of Weeks Dye Works floss in Tiger's Eye (brass)
- 1 skein *each* of DMC floss 333 (lavender) and 470 (mossy green)
- 10" x 12" piece of homespun for matting (optional)
- ¼" foam core for mounting
- Pigma Micron 03 black pen or very fine-point black permanent marker
- 8" x 9¼" frame (optional)★

★ *The frame shown was made by my husband, Tom Cross. The inside opening is 5" x 6¼" and the outside dimensions are 8" x 9¼".*

Drawing the Pattern

1. Photocopy or trace the pattern below. Note that the pattern is the reverse of how the witch appears in the project photograph because you'll be punching from the back side. The finished design will be facing the same way as in the photo.

2. Tape the pattern to a sunny window, and then tape the 12" square of weaver's cloth over the paper pattern. Make sure the weaver's cloth is centered over the pattern and on the straight of the grain.

3. Using the Pigma pen, trace the pattern onto the fabric.

Punching Order

Use three strands of floss throughout this project.

1. Outline and fill the witch. I used two strands of Black Crow and one strand of Tin Bucket together in the needle to outline and fill the witch.

2. Punch one row of Tiger's Eye around the entire perimeter of the design. Use Tiger's Eye to fill in the spots between the witch's arms and the broom handle.

3. Punch one row of green around the entire perimeter of the design. Follow that with one row of lavender.

4. Finish and frame the piece, referring to "Finishing Options" on page 37.

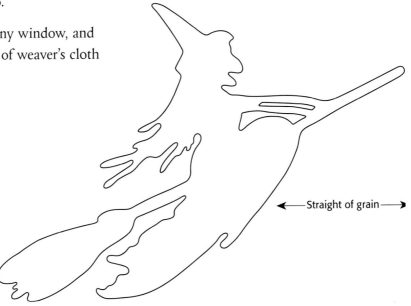

←— Straight of grain —→

Brunhilda pattern

SKEW BALLS

Skew Balls are my three-dimensional interpretation of the hooked rug Askew on page 50. They're so much fun to make. In my house they fill an old basket that sits on a dry sink. You could makes lots of them and fill a bread bowl. They also make great gifts for all the cats in your life.

Finished size: Approximately 1" to 3" in diameter

Materials

The materials given are enough to make 6 balls.

- 3 to 6 ounces of natural roving for ball cores
- 1 to 2 ounces *total* of dyed roving in colors of your choice for various designs
- 36-gauge felting needle
- Block of foam at least 2" thick

Directions

These directions will be used to make any of the skew balls. Sizes vary from Ping-Pong ball size to baseball size.

1. Use a wad of natural roving a little larger than the size ball you intend to make, and shape it in your hands as you would a snowball.

2. Place the ball on the foam block and start to poke the roving ball. Gradually turn the ball and continue poking until you have a firm, round shape.

3. Place small pieces of dyed roving on top of your skew ball one at a time. Poke the dyed roving onto the ball in any design you want, or see the "Design Options" box for ideas. Continue poking until the dyed wool is firmly in place.

Design Options

- **Polka dots.** Roll a small piece of dyed roving in your fingers to make a tiny little ball. Place the little wadded up balls on the larger ball and poke them into place.
- **Stripes.** Lay a thin strip of dyed roving around the ball to form a striped band. Poke it into place and add additional stripes in other colors as desired.
- **Christmas balls.** Make solid-colored red, white, and green balls, and fill a large crystal compote with them for a whimsical centerpiece.
- **Cat toys.** Place a bit of dried catnip in the center of the wad of natural roving before forming the core skew ball. Finish the ball with some brightly colored dyed wool and give it to your favorite cat.

What more can I say? I love pumpkins, bittersweet, mums, and spooky things that go bump in the night. The more pumpkins I can have at my house the better. And the beauty of these little pumpkins is that they're sure not to rot.

Approximate finished sizes:
 4¾" x 2" with 1¼" stem
 4" x 4¼" with 1½" stem
 3½" x 3¾" with ¾" stem

Materials

The materials given are more than enough to make all 3 pumpkins.

- 3 to 6 ounces of natural roving for pumpkin cores
- 2 to 3 ounces of dyed orange roving for pumpkins
- 1 ounce of dark brown natural roving for stems
- 36-gauge felting needle
- Block of foam at least 2" thick

Directions

1. Using your hands and a wad of natural roving a little larger than the size of the pumpkin you want to make, shape the roving into a short, squatty, or tall pumpkin. For the two-tiered pumpkin, make two separate shapes approximately the size of each pumpkin.

2. Place the pumpkin shape on the foam block and start to poke the roving. Gradually turn the pumpkin and continue poking until you have a firm shape that resembles the pumpkin you are aiming to make. Remember—pumpkins aren't perfect.

3. When you're happy with the shape of your pumpkin-to-be, start to layer on some orange roving and needle it in place. Continue doing this until the pumpkin is completely covered.

4. To form grooves on a pumpkin, use your needle and poke a curved line from about the top center of the pumpkin down to just about the bottom center. You may have to needle (or poke) over this line several times to get a nice deep ridge. Before you get carried away with the first groove, add several more grooves. Try and space them about the same distance apart, but don't worry if they aren't spaced equally. Go back over all the grooves to create a definite indentation where you want the grooves to be. (See the photo on page 42.)

5. Place a small piece of dark brown roving directly on the foam block. Poke it continuously until it resembles a stem. You should form it so the top of the stem is narrower than the bottom, which will be adhered to the top of the pumpkin. Place the stem in the center of the top of the pumpkin and slowly attach it by poking the dark brown stem into the orange base. It's amazing how easily it attaches.

6. For the two-tiered pumpkin, follow the directions above to make two small pumpkins. Once you like the way they look, attach the smaller of the two to the top of the larger one. Working around as you did with the stem, join the two pumpkins. Add the stem and a face if desired.

Face Making
- Roll small pieces of the dark brown roving into tiny balls. Apply these pieces to the front of the pumpkin and poke them into place where you want the eyes and nose to be, until they are secure.
- For the mouth, roll a piece of brown roving into a thin strip. Apply this to the face and poke it into place until it's secure.
- Instead of roving, try wool yarn to make facial features. It can be poked into place easily. Buttons make great eyes.
- If you want triangular features on your pumpkin, form them on your block of foam first. After you've shaped the features, peel them off the foam and apply them to the pumpkin.

This pillow is an example of flat needle felting. The roving is applied to a flat piece of wool. You can do so many things with flat needle felting, such as decorating Christmas stockings and wool vests, and making simple, little pillows like the project here.

Finished size: 13½" x 10¾"

Materials

- Fat quarter (18" x 22") of cotton home-spun fabric to complement your wool and bird color
- 12" square of beige wool
- 2 ounces of dyed red roving
- 1 ounce of dark brown natural roving
- 9" x 12" pillow form
- 36-gauge felting needle
- Block of foam at least 2" thick
- Red Dot Tracer
- Fine-point permanent marker

Felting the Bird

1. Trace the pattern on page 94 onto a piece of Red Dot Tracer.

2. Transfer the pattern from the Red Dot Tracer onto the piece of beige wool using a fine-point permanent marker.

3. Lay the beige wool over the foam block. Then apply a small amount of red roving to the wool, following the outline of the bird and making sure to cover the black outline. Fill in the bird with the red roving.

4. Roll small amounts of dark brown roving between your hands into thin rolls. Use these rolls for the legs, wing, and tail outlines. Use the felting needle to poke them until they adhere to the wool backing firmly.

5. Roll a small ball of dark brown roving and poke it into place for the bird's eye.

Assembling the Pillow

1. Trim your piece of wool with the needle-felted bird to 10" x 7¼".

2. Cut the homespun fabric into the following pieces:
   - 2 strips, 2½" x 10"
   - 2 strips, 2½" x 11¼"
   - 1 rectangle, 14" x 11¼"

3. With right sides together, use a ¼" seam allowance to sew the 2½" x 10" homespun strips to the top and bottom of the pillow front.

4. Sew the 2½" x 11¼" homespun strips to the sides of the pillow front in the same manner. The pillow top should now measure 14" x 11¼".

5. With right sides together, sew the pillow front to the piece of homespun that measures the same size. Sew around all four sides using a ½" seam allowance, leaving a 6" opening along the bottom center to slip the pillow form through.

6. After inserting the pillow form, slip-stitch the opening closed by hand.

Design Options
- Make a blue bird—or whatever color bird you like.
- Trace one of the flowers from your enlargement of the Bird among the Flowers rug on page 72 and make a flower pillow.
- Trim your pillow with wool rather than cotton homespun.

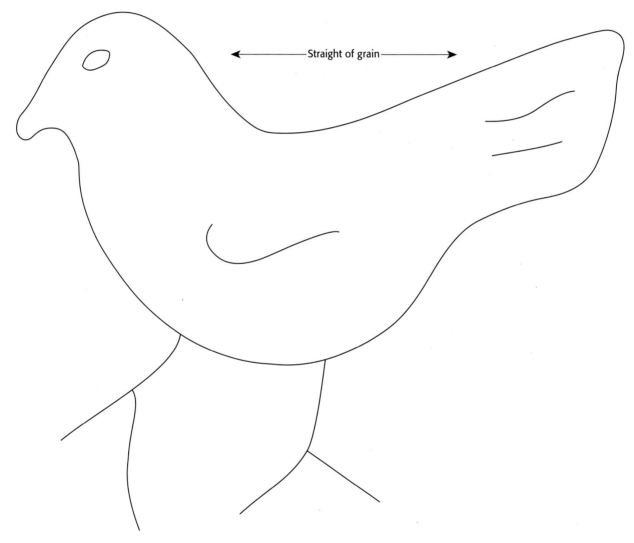

Straight of grain

Bird Pillow pattern

RESOURCES

Below are some excellent sources for all the equipment and supplies you'll need for the projects in this book. Three publications on rug hooking are also listed.

Suppliers of Cutters, Frames, Dyes, Yarn, and Wool

Blackberry Primitives
1944 High St.
Lincoln, NE 68502
402-421-1361
402-423-8464
www.blackberryprimitives.com

Dorr Mill Store
PO Box 88
Guild, NH 03754
800-846-DORR
www.dorrmillstore.com

Harry M. Fraser Company
PO Box 939
Stoneville, NC 27048
336-573-9830
www.fraserrugs.com

Mary Flanagan Woolens
470 County Rd. M
Pickett, WI 54964
920-589-2221
www.mfwoolens.com

Rigby Precision Products
PO Box 158
Bridgton, ME 04009
207-647-5679

Townsend Industries
PO Box 97
Altoona, IA 50009
877-868-3544
www.townsendfabriccutter.com

W. Cushing & Company
PO Box 351
Kennebunkport, ME 04046
800-626-7847
www.wcushing.com

The Wool Studio
706 Brownsville Road
Sinking Spring, PA 19608
610-678-5448
www.thewoolstudio.com

York Woolens
450 7th Ave., Suite 406
New York, NY 10123
800-303-0409
www.yorkfabrics.com

Magazines

Association of Traditional Hooking Artists (ATHA)
Joan Cahill, Membership Chairman
600½ Maple St.
Endicott, NY 13760
607-748-7588
www.atharugs.org

Rug Hooking Magazine
1300 Market St., Suite 202
Lemoyne, PA 17043
800-233-9055

The Wool Street Journal
312 Custer Ave.
Colorado Springs, CO 80903
888-RUG-LOOP
www.woolstreetjournal.com

Punchneedle Suppliers

Morgan Hoops & Stands Inc.
10025 Highway BB
Hillsboro, MO 63050-3408
314-540-1717
www.nosliphoops.com

The Needle Nook
Donna McDowell
100 E. Main St.
Ligonier, PA 15658
724-238-7874

Woolen Whimsies
Linda Repasky
19 Kettle Hill Rd.
Amherst, MA 01002
413-548-8040
www.woolenwhimsies.com

Needle-Felting Suppliers

Kindred Spirits
115 Colonial Ln.
Kettering, OH 45429
937-435-7758
www.kindredspiritsdesigns.com

The Woolery
PO Box 468
Murfreesboro, NC 27855
800-441-9665
www.woolery.com

PAT **CROSS** lives in Charlottesville, Virginia, with her husband, Tom, and their three cats, Emma, Molly, and Tucker. She has been designing and hooking rugs for over 15 years. By using her scrappy or "make-do" primitive style of hooking, Pat takes new rug patterns and makes them look like antiques. She has taught at private workshops and rug camps including the Green Mountain Rug School, Green Lake Rug Camp, and Shenandoah Valley Rug Retreat.

To share her love of rug hooking, Pat has published articles on dyeing, antique-looking scrappy rugs, and a judge's perspective in *Rug Hooking* magazine and *A Celebration of Hand-Hooked Rugs: Celebration XI*. She was the featured teacher in the March/April/May 2005 issue of *Rug Hooking* magazine. Pat also wrote *Purely Primitive: Hooked Rugs from Wool, Yarn, and Homespun Scraps* (Martingale & Company, 2003), contributed a hooked rug pattern in *Hooked on Wool: Rugs, Quilts, and More* (Martingale & Company, 2006), and a punchneedle pattern in *A Passion for Punchneedle* by Linda Repasky (Martingale & Company, 2006).

ACKNOWLEDGMENTS

First and foremost I want to thank everyone who bought my first book, *Purely Primitive: Hooked Rugs From Wool, Yarn, and Homespun Scraps*. It has made me very happy to see so many enjoy the book and get really hooked on rug hooking.

A big thank-you goes to the entire staff of Martingale & Company. These very creative people took what I sent them, photographed it, and then put all the pieces together to produce another beautiful publication.

Thank you, Kathy Parker, for welcoming the Martingale staff into your wonderful home to photograph the projects for this book. The setting couldn't have been better!

I could not have done this book without the help of my husband, Tom. He is my sounding board, my editor, my creative director, my computer guru, and my best friend. He keeps me sane and happy. I thank him for all his support, encouragement, and hard work.